The Pluralistic Economy

ELI GINZBERG

DALE L. HIESTAND

BEATRICE G. REUBENS

The Pluralistic Economy

New York

San Francisco

Toronto

London

Sydney

 McGRAW-HILL BOOK COMPANY

THE PLURALISTIC ECONOMY

For Gertrude D. Stewart,
counselor and friend to two generations
of fledgling Columbia economists

Preface

The Conservation of Human Resources Project of Columbia University, under a contract with the U.S. Department of Labor, initiated a series of studies in the fall of 1962 on "Manpower Resources and Economic Growth." In an attempt to learn about the relationships between the nation's manpower and the level of economic activity, the staff of the Conservation Project pursued different but related approaches. One was to appraise the extent of the recent expansion of employment in the not-for-profit sector, that is, in nonprofit institutions and in government. This volume on *The Pluralistic Economy* presents our findings growing out of this approach.

The second line of inquiry has been directed toward the analysis of a selected number of case studies illustrating the strategic role of manpower in the expansion of an industry. Two studies are nearing completion. The first is an analysis of *Manpower Resources and Nuclear Power;* the second is a study of *The Expansion of Business Services.*

Work has recently been initiated along a third axis. We are studying various dynamic constellations involved in the expansion of employment with the aim of unraveling the interrelations among the initial stimulus to expansion and the secondary and tertiary reinforcements. Our working title for this effort is *Varieties of Employment Expansion.*

A draft of the present book with the title *Expanding Employment in a Pluralistic Economy* was completed in the fall of 1963. A limited number of copies were distributed to government agencies and to research organizations for critical review. The Conservation staff acknowledges with sincere appreciation the assistance which it received from these reviews and discussions of its work with the U.S. Department of Labor, the Council of Economic Advisers, the National Bureau of Economic Research, and the Brookings Institution.

The Conservation staff also profited from the constructive recommendations of Prof. Moses Abramovitz of Stanford University, Prof. Sidney S. Alexander of the Massachusetts Institute of Technology, and Prof. Herbert E. Klarman of Johns Hopkins University. Dr. Victor Fuchs of the National Bureau of Economic Research submitted the draft manuscript to a page-by-page and line-by-line scrutiny. His detailed critique enabled us to improve the manuscript substantially.

Stanley Diller, Istvan B'Racz, and Dietrich Weismann, former members of the Conservation staff, were engaged on this project.

Several years ago Professsor Hiestand and I began a dialogue about the multiple ramifications of the shift of the American economy from the production of goods to the production of services. These explorations led us to focus on the not-for-profit economy. Professor Hiestand served as project director of the present study.

Chapter 7, Defense Contracting: Aerospace, first appeared in an extended version in *Law and Contemporary Problems, Government Contracts Part II,* vol. 29, no. 2, pp. 453–467, School of Law, Duke University, Spring, 1964, under the title: "Manpower Utilization in Aerospace."

Mrs. Roberta Handwerger helped in pulling together and updating the statistical data.

Ruth S. Ginzberg undertook the editorial revision.

The final draft of the manuscript was typed by Dolores Blaich, Sylvia Leef, and Virginia Stevens.

ELI GINZBERG, *Director*
Conservation of Human Resources Project

Contents

1

A Realistic Model

A quarter of a century ago, the great British economist John Maynard Keynes wrote that "practical men, who believe themselves to be quite exempt from any intellectual influences, are usually the slaves of some defunct economist." Keynes bemoaned the fact that the legislator and the executive were unable to breach the inevitable gap between the new and improved theory and the antiquated criteria for action that continued to serve as their guide.

Keynes's formulation about the state of theory and the shape of action can be made even more general. No statesman, conservative or liberal, can reach a determination about the desirability of a suggested policy or program unless he can fit it into his concept of the operation of the economy. It is therefore surprising that the concept of the American economy commonly held by businessmen, politicians, and academicians today is largely the same as that which has dominated the scene since the emergence of this nation as a

1

major industrial power toward the end of the nineteenth century.

This concept holds private profit-seeking enterprises to be almost solely responsible for the innovations and investments which are responsible for the constant broadening and deepening of the nation's economic activities. It holds that government plays a part, but a minor part, restricted primarily to setting and monitoring the rules which govern competition among private firms.

But this concept does not square fully with the facts, neither with the reality of yesteryear, nor with the conditions that prevail today. The three levels of government—Federal, state, and local—have always been engaged in the production of essential goods and services, ranging from the construction of navy vessels to the operation of schools. Of course, governments fulfill their economic functions in a manner different from that of private profit-seeking concerns, but these differences should not obscure the fact that governments engage in enterprise functions.

Similarly, there is another group of organizations engaged in performing useful functions, ranging from operating hospitals and universities to publishing religious books. They do not seek or make profits and do not obtain their revenues from taxes. These nonprofit institutions, like governments, are not subject to the full rigors of the competitive market, but they are nevertheless part of the nation's enterprise structure.

The conventional model of the economy concentrates on the private profit-seeking sector. A more realistic model suggests that there are three principal sectors of enterprise: profit-seeking, nonprofit, and government. Taken together, government and nonprofit constitute the not-for-profit sector. While this monograph will be built around an analysis of the not-for-profit sector, we want to point out that the American economy is in fact even more complex and that additional subsidiary categories can readily be identified.

There are three distinguishable and distinct forms of enterprise that do not fit appropriately into the profit, nonprofit, or conventional government sectors. First are the large private enterprises, engaged in transportation, communications, banking, insurance, and the production of power, whose operations are controlled by government agencies; these agencies usually determine the prices that can be charged and the profits that can be earned. These "public utilities" have long been the subject of study by academicians and have often been the center of dispute in the political arena; they represent a distinctive type of enterprise structure.

Another significant and distinguishable type can be subsumed under the heading "defense industries." The Armed Forces have always relied on purchases in the marketplace both for consumables and for weapons of war. During the last two decades, however, there has been a radical alteration in the pattern. A considerable number of companies, some with annual sales of as much as $2 billion, sell almost all of their output to the Department of Defense. What they produce, the time allowed for production, the detailed specifications of quality, as well as the prices that can be charged and the profits that may be retained are all determined by negotiation between the United States government and the company. In many instances, the facilities that the company uses, even its equipment and much of its know-how, have been

provided by the Federal government. These are not government enterprises; but neither are they conventional profit-
seeking enterprises. The major defense companies are a new
hybrid and represent a distinctive type of enterprise.

A third distinctive type that does not fit neatly into any of
the three major sectors is the government-subsidized private
enterprise which in turn must conform many of its operations to government criteria. This condition applies to parts
of the maritime industry, to feeder airlines, to selected mining companies, and to still others. An example of the way in
which government determines the detailed operations of
these subsidized companies is the Federal regulation that the
salaries of senior executives of subsidized shipping lines may
not exceed $25,000 annually.

Since there is a considerable literature dealing with public
utilities and since subsidized industries have also been the
subject of scholarly investigations, we shall give special attention only to the new defense industries. They represent a special type of profit-seeking enterprise in that almost all of
their sales are made to the Federal government to a point
where the decisions of bureaucrats, rather than their own
management, determine their profitability and even their
survival. But there are many other industries whose economic well-being is substantially affected by the efforts of the
community to meet its needs through the purchases of governmental nonprofit organizations.

Since the principal thrust of this analysis will be to highlight the significant enterprise activities carried on by the not-
for-profit sector—nonprofit institutions and government—it
may prove helpful to provide a little more illustrative material by way of a general introduction.

The Financial Report of Columbia University for 1962–1963 carries the information that the University had an income and operating expenses of more than $85 million. The Report states that "the University's operations constitute a sizable 'business' in any terms chosen to measure them...." While nonprofit institutions operate under certain special governmental privileges, the most important of which is their exemption from taxes, they are not governmental enterprises. Moreover, while they engage in the buying and selling of goods and services, they do not seek to make a profit, the chief proximate and ultimate aim of business enterprises.

For most purposes, the variegated economic activities carried on by governments under their own auspices are usually lumped together; only occasionally is a differentiation made between those goods and services made available by governments to the community at large through the use of the tax dollar and the goods and services that governments sell to consumers for a price. We seldom realize that governments also act like business concerns in mobilizing capital and other resources in order to produce goods or services as efficiently as possible with an aim to sell them to the consuming public, sometimes even at a price above cost, as in the operation of toll roads and liquor stores. But in point of fact these "business-like" activities of government are substantial: we see them in transportation, recreation, power, and many other areas.

The long-established and entrenched model of the economy, by focusing exclusively on profit-seeking activities of business concerns, carried with it the implication that private enterprises were considered primarily if not exclusively responsible for the growth of output and employment. The businessman's search for profits was held to be the key to economic development. The model made allowance for the fact that part of the profits of business is conventionally siphoned off by government in taxes so that the latter can provide diversified services to the community at large. The taxes that government levies directly on individual and corporate incomes as well as the indirect taxes that it collects on purchases and sales by businessmen and consumers are considered "withdrawals" from the main business stream. If consumers could retain more of the income they earn, they would be able to save more or to buy more of the products of industry. If corporations could retain more of their profits, they would be able to pay higher dividends or to invest more in new and improved plant and equipment which would in turn redound to the advantage of the public through better goods at lower prices.

The conventional view holds that when government gains control of a considerable portion of the private income through taxes, it diminishes the resources available to productive enterprises and thereby acts to slow the pace of economic expansion. The view rests on the basic assumption that most of what government does makes little or no direct, positive contribution to the nation's output or employment. However, let us consider briefly selected activities carried on by a large government agency.

The U.S. Department of Commerce collects and disseminates information about trade activities both at home and abroad; it operates the weather bureau; it provides grants and loans to various communities to speed their economic development; it runs a major testing and research laboratory. Private companies engaged in the collection and publishing of trade information, in the operation of laboratories, in investment banking are certainly considered enterprises in the conventional sense of the term: they corral scarce resources, combine them for useful purposes, and market the output in order to make a profit. Similarly, the U.S. Department of Commerce must obtain manpower and capital resources in order to perform its activities; it seeks to use them in an effective manner; it must distribute its output. It appears then that the Department of Commerce is engaged in economic activity. There are, of course, differences between the way a government enterprise secures its capital and decides on and distributes its output and the methods followed by a conventional business organization—and these differences are frequently important. Nevertheless the enterprise activities carried on by many government agencies—as well as those of nonprofit organizations such as universities, hospitals, cooperatives—all contribute to the gross national product.

The instrument manufacturer who sells a new piece of equipment to the Bureau of Standards, the manufacturer who sells electric typewriters to the Bureau of Foreign and Domestic Commerce, the corporation that sells large computers to the Bureau of the Census are equally willing to have as their customers the U.S. Department of Commerce, a nonprofit organization, or a private enterprise. Similarly, the secretary employed in a government agency receives a salary check which differs little if at all from that which she would receive if she were working for a private concern or a nonprofit organization. And the source of her income is a matter of no concern to her landlord, the local tradesmen, or the service station.

There is a complementary relation among the sectors of

the economy. The U.S. Department of Commerce entered upon the collection and dissemination of information about trade activities at home and abroad because the business community needed these data and encouraged Congress to appropriate funds for their collection. The Weather Bureau prepares essential services for many different business interests, particularly those engaged in the operation of airlines, resorts, outdoor sports events, and retail trade. The Department's special programs, established to assist communities to speed their economic development, recognize that if a local economy can be energized, many businessmen may increase their output and their sales and many workers may find jobs and increase their earnings. If the program is very successful, the additional taxes which government will receive will more than cover the costs of the special help which is extended. Finally, the work carried on by the Department in its Bureau of Standards provides crucially important information for a large number of different businesses, which reduces their risks and contributes to their profitability.

An even more striking example of the principle of complementarity among the sectors of the economy is provided by the automotive industry. There is a broad consensus that the nation's most dynamic industry is automotive manufacturing. When Detroit has a good year, it is likely that the economy is expanding; when Detroit is in the doldrums, the economy is likely to be dragging. However, the automotive industry could never have grown and prospered to such an extent had it not been for the willingness of state and, later, Federal legislators to appropriate very large sums for the construction and maintenance of a superior system of local roads and state and national highways. No amount of ingenuity in the private sector could have assured the success of the industry. Complementary activity by the governmental sector was essential.

It could almost be argued that one test of the competence of private entrepreneurs is their ability to get government to assure the growth and prosperity of their own industry. The automotive industry has demonstrated marked skill in the arena of public relations and in lobbying. But its efforts were aided by widespread consumer interest in improved roads and by the ability of legislators to find the financing. The concatenation could not have been more favorable: taxes levied on gasoline would underwrite much larger appropriations for roads; rural communities would gain both from an economic and social point of view; and large-scale construction and continuing maintenance would provide a considerable amount of part-time employment for many farming communities. What greater bonanza could rural legislators ask for!

Another striking case of complementary activity involves nuclear power, which by the end of this century may account for more than half of the nation's total stationary power. The scientific work underlying the new technology was conducted in nonprofit institutions—in the universities at home and abroad. The second stage involved the tremendous commitment of the United States government during World War II in connection with the atomic bomb. The Federal government through the Atomic Energy Commission continued to play the dominant role until 1954, when opportunities were opened for the first time to the private sector. In the past decade, electrical manufacturing companies, several aerospace companies, an increasing number of public utilities, and more recently even chemical companies have entered the field in the hope and expectation of making profits from one or another stage in the production and sale of nuclear power. But even as the private sector became much more heavily involved, the Federal and, to a lesser extent, state governments have continued to play a constructive role through subsidizing research and development, making plans and strategic materials available free or below cost, undertaking training programs, providing special insurance, and a great many other supportive actions.

These examples of complementary activity could be multiplied: the educational efforts of the agricultural extension service and the expansion of farm machinery and fertilizer companies, the symbiosis between the broadening and deepening of public education and the expansion of book publishing, the military programs of the Federal government and the expansion of the airplane industry. Since nonprofit and governmental institutions are responsible for the education and training of most of the nation's professional, technical, and managerial manpower, it could be argued that the ability of the private sector to operate and expand is directly dependent on the efficiency with which these sectors perform their basic training missions.

Another basic consideration that must be introduced in order to establish a realistic model of the contemporary economy relates to the interdependency and competition among the several markets. This has been suggested, but it must now be made explicit. Enterprises in the different sectors—profit, nonprofit, and government—draw from the same resource pools of men and money; they frequently sell their output in the same markets; and they may compete with each other for a preferred position with respect to expanding their operations.

In June of each year there is active competition among the Federal, state, and local civil service commissions, private employers, and educational, research, and other types of nonprofit organizations for college graduates and for those who have secured their master's degrees or their doctorates. Similar competition exists in other manpower markets. When the Veterans Administration raised their pay scale for nurses some years ago, voluntary hospitals in many communities complained that the Federal government was "spoiling the market." Many of their staff nurses resigned to accept employment in a neighboring Veteran's Administration hospital. In both blue- and white-collar work there is continuing competition among all three sectors for the same skilled personnel, be they plumbers or secretaries.

The three sectors also compete in money as well as in manpower markets. Since local and state governments finance most of their capital programs through bond issues, they usually have recourse to the same lending institutions from which the private sector seeks funds. A state or municipality, a college or a hospital, and private corporations frequently compete for the same funds. The profit, nonprofit, and governmental sectors also compete with each other in the distribution and sale of some of their goods and services. New York City has a large municipal hospital system, a still larger aggregation of beds in voluntary hospitals, and a significant number of proprietary hospitals. Consequently, during periods of the year when there are many vacant hospital beds, physicians and others who influence hospital admissions may be under pressure to send their patients to a specific institution.

Similar types of competition exist in other areas. We find it in the educational arena at every level from kindergarten to professional education. It is also found in some degree even in commodity production. In several areas of the country, Federal or state agencies sell electric or other power in competition with private enterprise. Conflicts have recently arisen between the Port of New York Authority and certain private real estate interests. The latter fear that if the Port Authority proceeds with its plans to erect two new skyscrapers as part of a world trade center and if it succeeds in enticing government agencies to relocate in its new center, they will lose tenants whom they will be unable to replace. Other landlords look with favor on the plan because of the increases in business that they anticipate in the neighborhood of the new trade center.

We have seen that the prevailing view of the American economy is that it grows and prospers in response to the dynamism of the private sector. The burden of the foregoing pages has been to complicate this model of the contemporary economy by calling attention to the significant enterprise role played by the two other sectors—government and nonprofit. We must still decide whether their role is new or whether it is the recognition of their role which is new. The answer is that government and nonprofit organizations have long played an important role in the development of the American economy. It was only sixteen years after the settlement of the Massachusetts Bay Colony in the New World that Harvard College was established as a nonprofit institution for the training of an educated leadership. For a long time higher education was overwhelmingly under the control of nonprofit institutions and even today these institutions, while sharing responsibility with state governments, continue to play a very important role.

The large-scale capital investments in inland water transportation were initiated and carried out primarily by state agencies. The development of the railroads was assisted by the land grants and other types of aid that the promoters received from Federal, state, and local governments. One stimulus to a modern textile industry in the South after the Civil War was the successful effort of various communities to raise the capital required to provide employment opportunities for the surplus white population. A careful review of the record would point up a large number of other governmental enterprises: local hospital systems, gas and electrical plants, water systems, arsenals, shipyards, lumbering and mining operations, and many more. Similarly, many different types of activity, in addition to higher education, that were entered into and long carried on by nonprofit organizations include the operation of hospitals, grain elevators, farming, banking, insurance.

It may be true that the key to our economic development is in the dynamism of the private sector, but the historical record is unequivocal about the fact that many governmental and nonprofit organizations also have long been engaged in enterprise. The relative weight of these sectors is vastly greater today than heretofore, such that one may speak of a veritable transformation of the economy, but their participation in the economic life of America goes back to colonial times.

So far the focus has been primarily on the government's role in the nation's economic activities. And this analysis will continue to focus on these activities. However, government exercises a great many powers which have a potent influence on the shape and direction of the nation's economic life. This is true with regard to the Federal government's monetary and fiscal policies, tariffs, antitrust activities, income maintenance and income transfer programs, and patent and trademark laws. At the state and local level, note should be taken of the tax system, building codes, the right of eminent domain, mortgage activities, and many more. An assessment of government's wide-ranging financial, regulative, and related policies on the operation of economy will not be undertaken in this investigation. We are concerned rather with the economic resources used and the institutional relationships which are involved in the activities carried on by government as well as nonprofit institutions.

A few statistics will suggest the economic significance of these activities of government and nonprofit institutions. Education is one of the nation's largest industries, and it is carried on overwhelmingly outside of the private sector. Approximately one out of every three persons in the United States above school-entering age is a student. The health industry directly employs 2.5 million persons and accounts for an annual expenditure of almost $40 billion. At the fulcrum of this industry are the voluntary hospitals and the nonprofit insurance plans.

The Federal government's expenditures for defense, atomic energy, and space approximate $60 billion. Millions of persons are directly employed by the Department of Defense, and more millions have jobs with defense contractors solely because of the determination of the Federal government to maintain strong defense policies and to push ahead in the exploration of space and in the application of nuclear power.

It can be put another way. More people are directly employed in government than in agriculture, mining, and construction combined. The rate of growth of direct employment in the not-for-profit sector when added to the jobs in the private sector, supported by purchases of the not-for-profit sector, exceeded in each of the last three decades the gains of employment in the private sector. In the decade 1950–1960, nine out of every ten net new jobs added to the economy reflected, directly and indirectly, the activities of the not-for-profit sector.

These few facts indicate that we must broaden our model of the economy to make room for a consideration of non-profit and governmental enterprise activities; that even though these two sectors do not operate to make a profit, they are an integral part of the nation's enterprise structure; that it is not feasible to consider the operations of any one sector of the economy without understanding its complementary relations to the other sectors; that the three sectors draw their resources and generally sell their output in the same markets; that the profit, government, and nonprofit sectors have been existing side by side from the very beginnings of our history; and finally, that the not-for-profit sector has accounted for an increasing share of the nation's total economic activity.

2

The Three Sectors

The models that men use determine both their thoughts and their actions. As we noted in the preceding chapter, the accepted model of the American economy has long been one of a system of private enterprise. The prevailing doctrine has held that economic development results from private enterprises competing in free markets for the consumer's dollars. The successful make high profits; the unsuccessful go bankrupt. This simple model has been refined to make allowance for the fact that many concerns operate under conditions of imperfect competition. In a great many industries including steel, chemicals, automobiles, cigarettes, and pharmaceuticals, the individual enterprise regulates its price and output less with respect to the market as a whole than to the possible actions and reactions of a limited number of competitors. But this is a refinement of the competitive model, not a major extension or revision of it.

While the conventional model placed primary stress on the

private sector, it did include a role, however modest, for government. There has been general acceptance of the view that government is in a preferred position to provide certain basic services, such as education, public health, highways, postal system, more effectively and efficiently than any other agency of society. But the scale and scope of these services was minimized. They were not held to account for a significant share of the nation's total economic effort.

This singular image not only minimizes the economic activities carried on outside of the profit sector but pictures this sector as operating under a distinctive and unique set of incentives and pressures that do not apply to either government or nonprofit institutions. The dominant view holds that private enterprises are established and operated by entrepreneurs who, perceiving an opportunity to make money, provide or borrow the necessary capital; bid in the open market for, or develop on their own, specialized resources of men and materials; sell their products or services (ranging from the essential to the desirable, luxurious, or frivolous) to individual consumers or business concerns in competitive markets; and retain as profits the difference, if any, between their sales and their costs. Entrepreneurs always face uncertainty at each point in the process because the technology which they use and market relationships to which they are exposed are constantly shifting. The primary challenge that the businessman faces is to anticipate these changes by devising ways of reducing his costs and developing new products and markets.

By contrast, governmental agencies are usually considered to be bureaucratic organizations with clearly defined and more or less stable functions. But as the insidious term bureaucracy suggests, there is an assumption that these government agencies operate without any real management. It is assumed that minor appointed officials keep the wheels turning, subject of course to some loose controls from an elected executive, such as the President, governor, or mayor, and further by the fiscal and other powers exercised by legislative bodies. Instead of competent management, there is an admixture of political appointees, inefficient civil servants, and underpaid but dedicated specialists. These government agencies provide essential services to the community free of charge. Such services, it is said, cannot be obtained from private firms, primarily because entrepreneurs are unable or unwilling to risk the large amount of capital required or because they would not be able to sell these services to consumers at a price that would cover their costs. As a result, the costs of producing these services must be met ultimately by general or specific taxes imposed on the community at large.

Inherent in this popular conception of the contrast between the private and government sectors is the conviction that the "real" output of the economy, the goods and services that consumers and business want and need, reflects the economic activity carried on by the profit-seeking enterprises. It is widely believed that much of the activity in the government sector is unproductive, unnecessary, wasteful.

This picture is sharply drawn. It overstates current attitudes and values. Yet it is the model commonly used in current discussions about our economic system, the way in which it operates, and the conditions affecting its growth. This model dominates discussion in the political arena, and also serves as the analytical framework for many economists.

More sophisticated examiners include in their analysis the

contributions to total economic activity that arise in the government sector. But their manner of including these contributions indicates resistance to considering the government sector in the same way as the private sector. For instance, the Office of Business Economics of the U.S. Department of Commerce, which has responsibility for publishing the basic national income accounts, estimates the economic contribution of government solely in terms of the wages and salaries that government agencies pay their employees. No allowance is made for the value of land, buildings, or other capital resources that government agencies have used in producing services which are later distributed or sold to the public. In calculating the output of the private sector, national income analysts always take into account the capital used in producing the goods and services that are eventually sold. No account is taken, however, of rent paid, supplies used, or capital depreciated in producing the government's output.

There are other conventions in the national income accounts which also operate to reduce the significance of the government's role in the nation's total economic effort. For instance, the accounts show only the net balance between the subsidies advanced and the net surpluses earned by various government enterprises. This convention understates, by concentrating on a net financial balance, the total economic activity carried on by these agencies of government. In addition a significantly large amount of governmental purchases and expenditures is represented as expenditures by consumers. Although government is responsible for initiating various types of economic transactions, such as awarding research contracts to universities, the national income accounts show these expenditures by government as purchases by consumers, and the expenditures of nonprofit organizations are treated as consumer expenditures. While it is always difficult to trace the contribution of any sector, and while experts continue to disagree about preferred methods of handling certain items, one general observation can be made. The conventions which the specialists follow are consistently biased toward understating the contribution of the government sector to total national output.

This minimizing of government's economic activities has not been limited to the statistics of national income. It has been much more general and pervasive. For instance, there is widespread criticism of the expansion of government payrolls, but no serious effort has been made to consider this expansion in relation to the new and expanded services that the public has been demanding and obtaining in the fields of education, health, recreation. Similarly, while businessmen and government officials have been fully aware of the significance of defense contracts for the future welfare of the companies and communities in which they are interested, the ramifications of these defense contracts for the development of local, state, and regional economies have not been integrated with the analysis of the economy as a whole.

Nevertheless, our understanding of the government sector is considerably in advance of our knowledge of the nonprofit sector, which has seldom been studied and never exhaustively. Part of the difficulty lies in the fact that the category "nonprofit" is very broad and includes a great diversity of institutions, no one of which is typical of the sector as a whole. However, the sector is dominated by health and education activities.

The following listing suggests the variety of institutional

forms that fall legally within the nonprofit sector, although here we are mainly concerned with those which are enterprises producing goods and services for the public.

1. Mutual insurance companies
2. Savings and loan associations
3. Trade associations
4. Chambers of commerce
5. Professional societies
6. Farmers' cooperatives
7. Consumers' cooperatives
8. Trade unions
9. Private colleges or universities
10. Foundations
11. Voluntary hospitals
12. Research organizations
13. Churches
14. Social clubs
15. Blue Cross and Blue Shield insurance programs
16. Museums and libraries

Nonprofit institutions can be considered as falling between government at the one extreme and profit-seeking enterprises at the other. But many aspects of nonprofit institutions remain to be clarified. They are often considered "private" because they are not a part of government and have none of the powers of governments. On the other hand, they are often considered "public" because they serve a public purpose. Since they are considered to be more responsive to community than to personal goals, they are granted certain privileges. Whether an enterprise is designated as profit or nonprofit determines whether or not it must pay income, property, and other taxes; whether gifts or donations which it receives are deductible from gross income in determining the donors' tax liability; whether it is liable for contributions for unemployment compensation and social security for its work force; whether it is obliged to bargain with unions; whether it receives special mailing privileges; and whether it is eligible for other types of government assistance, such as surplus property.

Just as the conventional national income accounting procedures do not accurately reflect the scope of government operations, neither do they adequately present the scope of economic activities carried on by the nonprofit sector. The conventions in use tend to minimize the economic operations carried on by nonprofit organizations. For example, the money received by voluntary hospitals from government, commercial insurance, Blue Cross, and various welfare funds, in payment for hospitalization, is considered a consumer expenditure. The logic back of this convention is that nonprofit organizations exist to accomplish certain broad communal objectives. They are viewed as facilitating devices, not as organizations with independent purposes and goals. If this same approach were followed in national income accounting for private enterprises, there would be no expenditures by business firms!

Many nonprofit organizations perform functions that are identical or closely allied to those performed by government. In fact, many governments weigh carefully whether to establish or expand certain activities under their own aegis; whether to seek to accomplish their goals by relying on nonprofit organizations; or whether, as frequently happens, to do part of the work themselves and to look to nonprofit organizations to do the rest. Many large cities provide nursing and housekeeping services for the indigent sick, while similar services are provided by various nonprofit medical and health associations concerned with assisting patients stricken by cancer, tuberculosis, infantile paralysis, or still other serious chronic diseases. In order to provide hospital services to the indigent poor, New York City, in addition to operating a large municipal hospital system, pays for the care of considerable numbers of indigent patients in various voluntary hospitals.

In providing institutional care for children who for one reason or another cannot live with their parents, many communities rely exclusively on voluntary organizations. The municipality may pay full, or occasionally, even more than full operating costs. The logic back of this arrangement is twofold. There is a deeply ingrained negativism in many sections of the country toward expanding the operating functions of government; and there is a strong desire among various religious minorities to assume direct responsibility for the care of their young.

In other instances, while nonprofit and governmental units share in the performance of a particular community function, they may remain without an effective relationship. For a long time public and parochial school systems have been separate. In some areas, even formal communications between these two systems have been avoided, although the actions of one system have a direct effect on the other. The degree of attendance at parochial schools often has a major influence on the attitudes of the electorate with regard to support for public schools. Where there is no strong parochial school system, the public schools must provide most of the required educational facilities. In other areas the two systems are somewhat intertwined. Local and state educational authorities increasingly provide bus transportation, medical examinations, school lunch programs, and other general services for parochial as well as for public school students. Federal aid for student guidance, dormitory construction, and many other basic educational functions is currently available not only to public school systems but also to schools operated under religious or other "nonprofit" auspices.

The designation of an institutional form as profit, nonprofit, or governmental reflects primarily its legal ownership and only secondarily its economic operations or social purpose. However, various enterprises change with time, and this has been reflected by national income accounting, which conventionally treats mutual insurance companies, savings and loan associations, and cooperatives as business enterprises. Such enterprises were initially self-help institutions closely allied to charitable undertakings. With time, they became commercialized and now nearly all of them serve the general public. The consumer decides to use such an institution for precisely the same reasons which impel him to use any other type of commercial establishment. Currently, these originally self-help institutions rely overwhelmingly on paid employees; their management consists of executives chosen by self-perpetuating boards of directors. At some point in their development, these institutions began to resemble profit-seeking corporations despite their different legal basis. The modern corporation is likewise the product of an evolutionary process. The large corporation is today under the effective control of a hired management who are responsible for most of the major decisions. The owners are outsiders who often receive a fairly constant rate of return on their ownership shares—not unlike a depositor in a savings bank. They are treated by the management as another interest group similar to suppliers or dealers where stability in long-term relationships looms as a major objective.

In some nonprofit organizations such as trade associations, chambers of commerce, trade unions, professional societies, and even government agencies, various individuals or groups frequently operate in their own interests. To the extent that they do, they might be said to resemble "profit-seekers." To illustrate: It is common for various business concerns to band together as a "pressure group," as members of an *ad hoc* organization or in an established trade association, for the specific purpose of increasing their leverage in the market, either through direct economic action or indirectly through influencing consumer behavior or governmental action. Although the nonprofit organization makes no effort to realize specific monetary gains, it provides the instrumentality through which the participating members of the organization can seek to enlarge their profits. When a nonprofit organization representing a group of producers of petroleum products tries to reduce the import quotas set by the United States government, it is hoping to enlarge the share of the national market commanded by its member firms and subsequently enlarge their profits.

While the nonprofit American Medical Association has a great many social objectives in its program, the United States Supreme Court has indicated in a recent opinion that one important aim of the AMA has been to exercise monopolistic control over the supply and utilization of physicians with an aim of enhancing the earnings of its members. Paraphrasing Adam Smith, we can say that every nonprofit organization concerned with the economic environment of its participating members has as one of its primary objectives the enhancement of their personal gain.

There is another respect in which all types of institutions, nonprofit and governmental as well as profit-seeking, provide opportunities for key individuals to advance. In each sector, there is a hierarchy of jobs: some pay more than others, and some carry more prestige. Men move from the presidency of a small college to become the head of a larger university, as did Dr. Pusey when he left Lawrence College for Harvard University. Similar moves are made by hospital administrators, officers in the Armed Forces, city managers, executive directors of welfare organizations. The man who presides over an organization with large or expanding assets, income, expenditures, and personnel is likely to receive a high salary and other perquisites. Not long ago the press reported that a man, recently appointed bishop, had made his mark as the successful manager of the Church's rapidly expanding real estate holdings.

There is another facet that warrants comment. Executives in any of the three sectors are not necessarily confined to one sector throughout their careers. Upon their retirement, many senior officers of the Armed Forces secure top positions in American business. Occasionally they assume, as General Eisenhower did, the leadership of a major nonprofit institution. The Congress has found it necessary to pass special legislation to restrict the freedom of former Federal officials who worked in the Internal Revenue Service or in military procurement to accept positions in the profit-seeking sector which would make use of their specialized knowledge and connections. Few individuals who leave senior governmental positions have difficulty in securing desirable positions in the private sector of the economy.

The tenuousness of many conventional categories and distinctions is revealed when one recognizes that certain governmental operations have many of the characteristics of a profit-making enterprise. Many toll roads realize incomes far in excess of their capital and operating costs. So have many bridges, airports, auditoriums, convention centers, and other public installations. With the repeal of prohibition, a number of states established a statewide system of profit-making liquor stores. While the original aim may have been to exercise social control over the sale of intoxicating liquors, the continuation of state ownerships reflects the disinclination of the governmental authorities to forego such a lucrative source of income.

Finally, as noted earlier, certain types of "private" enterprise, particularly gas, electric, transportation, and communications companies, operate subject to governmental controls over their rates and profits. The existence or survival of other industries may actually be directly linked to special governmental programs or legal enactments or administrative provisions.

The interrelationships between governments and private enterprises which derive from government contracts and the large-scale purchases of governments raise additional questions about conventional distinctions between public and private profit-seeking organizations. In some industries and companies, sales to governmental units are only an incidental aspect of their total activities. In others, sales to government may be an important determinant of the industry's growth and prosperity. For instance, in the manufacture of school furniture or the provision of school transportation, government is the major market, but since there are tens of thousands of independent governmental units, the private entrepreneur may have considerable freedom. Some publishers of textbooks gear their sales to a national market and seek to eliminate any material that may be found objectional. Others look to a regional market and deliberately favor a Southern or Northern point of view.

Other businesses or industries exist solely or largely to serve one particular function of one particular governmental unit. The aircraft, shipbuilding, and uranium processing industries are substantially dependent on the Federal government. The scale of these enterprises, whether they are able to expand or forced to contract, as well as the level of profits that they are able to earn or the losses which they must absorb, is almost completely the result of governmental decisions.

Many industries were established that were able to survive only behind high tariff walls. Others, such as shipping lines and local airlines, exist only by virtue of sizable subsidies. The profitability of the oil industry has been greatly influenced by special depletion allowances. Stockpiling led to the establishment and expansion of many mining companies. Farm support programs provide the economic base for many farmers. Many builders have succeeded because of liberal mortgage money made available by government.

In certain segments of the construction industry—for instance, firms that specialize in the construction of schools, post offices, jails, highways, and dams—dependence on government is also substantial, although these companies are likely to deal with multiple governmental agencies at Federal, state, and local levels. Moreover, they frequently are also simultaneously engaged in work for other customers.

There are other instances of heavy economic dependence of private enterprises on government. Many cities and states have sought to broaden their economic base by offering to build or rent buildings to industrial companies on extremely favorable terms. Airline, bus, and trucking companies utilize terminals built by Federal, state, or local governments. Large-scale government financing for research and development programs underlies the changing technology in many industries, including aircraft, electronics, and nuclear power. In many cities, professional athletic clubs use municipal stadiums, which actually were built primarily for them.

This considerable intermingling among the several sectors of the economy does not obliterate all differences among profit-seeking enterprises, nonprofit organizations, and governmental agencies and enterprises. But the conventional distinctions among the sectors frequently conceal more than they reveal. There are a great many similarities among units in the different sectors, and we can legitimately consider the units in each of the sectors as enterprises organized for productive effort.

The key difference between the private sector and the not-for-profit sector is not in the economic activities which they undertake, but in whether they are organized in order to seek a profit from their efforts. Even this difference is not universal for, as we noted earlier, some governments—and some nonprofit organizations—operate with the intention of securing prices in excess of their costs.

Further evidence of similarities among the sectors can be found in their behavior in capital markets, in pricing, and in their fields of specialization. Although we conventionally think of private enterprises as bidding for funds competitively against other borrowers in the capital markets, important aircraft companies have received a considerable part of their capital as outright gifts or loans from government. Many governments, in contrast, are forced to seek funds for various programs by recourse to the capital markets where they must compete with other borrowers.

Typically, the prices of products produced by private enterprises are set by the competitive forces operating in the markets in which these products are sold. But in many instances large corporations are able to exercise substantial control over their prices. On the other hand, many government enterprises such as colleges, hospitals, toll roads, transit systems, and recreational undertakings must set their prices with an eye on their competitors.

While a distinction is often made between the social and economic utility of the goods and services produced by private enterprises and those provided by nonprofit organizations, the facts disclose a wide overlap. All three types of enterprises engage in the production of such basic services as communications, transportation, power, education, medical services.

The finding of the high order of interrelationship and mutual dependence among the three sectors of the economy provides the foundation for the chapters which follow. The next two set forth the proliferation of the types of governmental and nonprofit enterprises. The following two chapters provide statistical measures of the changing contributions to expenditures and employment provided by the profit and the not-for-profit sectors. These are followed by two case

studies—one of the new relations between government and
the profit sector (aerospace), the other of the expansion of a
nonprofit industry (health and medical services). The concluding chapter on enterprise and employment seeks to explore the extent to which adjustments in the relationships
among the three sectors are a precondition for meeting the
latent and overt needs and desires of the consuming public.
No one sector can service the public by itself. Therefore, we
must seek to identify the barriers to innovation and expansion and make the adjustments which will speed the growth
of employment and the effective utilization of human and
other resources.

3

Varieties of Governmental Enterprises

The preceding chapters have postulated that any organization which can corral scarce resources of men and matériel and organize them for the purpose of producing commodities or services for distribution or sale to the consuming public is engaged in productive economic activity. Therefore a more inclusive concept of this economy requires an understanding of the multiple economic activities in which government engages.

Political preference aside, economists generally agree that government's direct participation in the economy is likely to reflect the inability or unwillingness of private interests to provide certain goods and services that the community requires or desires, from national defense to the preservation of a wilderness preserve. While governments may be precipitated into various types of economic enterprise on a variety of grounds, the basic but by no means sole reason is the diffusion of benefits which makes it impossible for a private entrepreneur to sell his output to specific customers at a profitable price. The individual citizen cannot pay in the marketplace for his share of the missiles that help protect the United States, nor for his share of the public health program that undertakes the vaccination of all citizens against smallpox.

The utilization of economic resources by government has involved both the regular departments of government and the establishment of a large number of new governmental enterprise structures. It has also led to many new relationships between government and the other sectors, private profit-seeking enterprises and nonprofit organizations. This chapter will delineate some of the new forms of government enterprise in order to provide a background for understanding the comprehensive role that government has come to play in the operation of the economy. These extensions of government, beyond its conventional activities of defense, justice, and highways, date from long ago.

It is interesting to recall that New York State ventured into an area that had previously been dominated by private enterprise when it constructed the Erie Canal in 1817, after private companies had failed to improve inland navigation. The state did not hesitate to raise capital from private lenders, to apply general tax revenues to help meet construction costs, to charge tolls, and later to invest the receipts in the construction of other state canals. American history is rich in new forms of governmental enterprise as well as new forms of cooperation between government and the other sectors of the economy.

Nevertheless, the innovations in the forms of government

enterprise during the past several decades have been so varied and pervasive that they almost represent a structural transformation. Under the impact of depression, war, cold war, breakthroughs in nuclear power and in the technology of space, together with the intensification of problems precipitated by industrialization and urbanization, government has been brought face to face with new and demanding problems requiring attention and solution. As our history would have foretold, the response has been largely pragmatic. New departures have been made in enterprise forms as well as in their relations to private and nonprofit sectors, in Federal, state, and local governments. These innovations have resulted in an erosion of many conventional distinctions between the private enterprise and the governmental sector; they have led to the establishment of new joint forms of enterprises involving government and business, government and nonprofit organizations, and various levels of government; finally, they have resulted in a great proliferation of special-purpose public authorities or public corporations.

Whatever the reason that government enters upon a particular type of economic activity, we want to consider now the diversity of arrangements which governments may employ to carry out their functions as entrepreneurs. At one extreme is the classic approach: a government department receives an appropriation from the legislature to provide a service for the entire community, or for a substantial segment; it hires personnel and obtains other resources necessary to fulfill the specific function and it makes its services available to all who want it without charge. At the opposite extreme a government may establish a largely autonomous authority which is authorized to proceed with the production of certain desirable services, but which must resort to the capital markets for its long-term funds and secure its operating income from the charges which it levies. Such authorities may, and in fact often do, price their services so that they receive a margin above costs, even after allowance is made for depreciation and interest payments. Except for its lack of stockholders, its exemption from paying taxes, and its obligation to observe certain legal and administrative rules and regulations, the operations of such a government authority may be almost indistinguishable from that of a private concern.

In fact, many governments have come to operate in fields that are attractive to private enterprises and nonprofit organizations—such as hospitals, liquor stores, and technical training institutions. The overlap and competition between government and private enterprises is marked in shipbuilding, recreational activities, urban transportation, electric power production, and many other fields. There is an overlap between government and nonprofit institutions, particularly in education and hospitals, but also in research, health and welfare programs, guidance and counseling, housing and urban renewal projects.

There is no single explanation that fits all these overlaps. The prevailing ideology about government's role has long been that government should provide only those services required by the community which private enterprise or nonprofit organizations are unable or unwilling to undertake or which they cannot provide as well.

But this overstates the case. Significant differences in the strength of this ideology can be found depending on circumstances, time, and place. Hence the role of government in the economy shows considerable variation from one state to another, from one decade to the next.

Whether or not government is forced to act frequently depends on the strength of private and nonprofit institutions. In Rhode Island, government provides only about three-quarters of the elementary and secondary education; the parochial schools provide the rest. In South Carolina, private schools account for only 2 percent of the total; 98 percent of the responsibility devolves on government. The system of county hospitals in California bespeaks in part the absence of strong voluntary hospitals such as are found on the East Coast and which have long provided a considerable amount of free patient care.

On occasion, the government agency with primary responsibility for providing a certain service may not meet adequately the needs or desires of certain groups of citizens. This creates opportunities for private enterprise even in such fields as refuse removal or the protection of property and persons. Many restaurants and other institutions use private garbage-collection services, and many institutions contract with private companies to provide guards.

On occasion a government takes over private enterprise engaged in providing an essential service because the owner can no longer continue to operate efficiently or effectively. This was the predicament which New York City faced when the Fifth Avenue Coach Line collapsed. Sometimes government transfers activities to private enterprise. In recent years the Federal government, under the promptings of the first and second Hoover Commission, sold a large number of enterprises that it had earlier established or bought in order to meet certain specialized conditions, particularly the needs of the population on military posts in isolated areas. Time had operated to reduce their isolation, so that they now had access to services in the private economy.

Public enterprises are established at various levels of government: Federal, state, county, municipality, township and town, school district and special district. On occasion, government enterprises are established through the cooperation of two or more governments at the same level. They can develop as the result of cooperative action between different levels of government. Public enterprises at different governmental levels often offer similar types of services, such as in national, state, county, city, and town parks. Hospitals are another illustration.

The Federal government operates important economic activities through conventional departments as well as through independent agencies. The activities carried on by the Post Office or in the shipyards owned and operated by the Navy closely resemble activities carried on by private business. The Government Printing Office is another business-type operation. An outstanding innovation in government enterprise forms was the Tennessee Valley Authority. Mingling commercial power production and transmission, nonprofit community services and governmental flood control efforts, TVA applied massive doses of capital to develop an entire region under a multipurpose program. No agency or company without the right of eminent domain and without access to large amounts of free or low-interest capital could have undertaken such an ambitious task. As a federally financed enterprise, TVA was able to tap resources from the entire country and use them to assist a particular underdeveloped region. Some have argued that while good for the region, this kind of action may have such deleterious effects on other regions that the net social costs may outweigh net social benefits. The thrust of this argument has been sufficient to stop Congress from embarking on equally ambitious projects and to place restrictions on the scale of TVA's further expansion.

At the state level, various turnpike and bridge authorities represent substantial public enterprises. The New Jersey Turnpike and the Pennsylvania Turnpike are independent, self-financing entities, which charge tolls sufficient to repay the money borrowed for the original capital investment, to cover operating and maintenance costs, and to yield significant surpluses. These turnpike revenues and surpluses are sufficiently large in New Jersey that the Governor sought approval recently to pledge them for educational expansion. State liquor stores are another type of self-financing enterprise which yields surpluses above the costs of operation.

On the other hand, state mental hospitals and state universities are large enterprises which make no effort to recover their operating costs and certainly not their full costs. In California, tuition and fees account for only 4 to 5 percent of the operating budget for public higher education. The citizens of that state strongly believe that irrespective of the advantages that accrue to the individual, higher education yields so many diffuse benefits that the costs should be a charge against the general revenues of the state. In New York, payments by and on behalf of patients total only about 10 percent of the operating budget of the state mental hospital system. It is recognized that since some patients may be confined to a mental hospital for very long periods, even for the whole of their natural lives, most families would find the cost of paying for them exceedingly onerous, if not totally impractical.

About fifty municipalities own and operate transportation systems. The New York City Transit Authority is the largest, with annual revenues of about $287 million. Municipal or other local governmental gas and electric power enterprises are common throughout the country, though they rarely are in direct competition with private enterprises. Their existence, however, usually tends to keep private enterprise from entering the locality. School districts, with their elected, non-political school boards, are important government enterprise units. They employ large numbers of persons and compete with one another in hiring teachers and other personnel. They purchase from the private economy large quantities of supplies, books, furniture, bus services, architects' services, building materials, etc. Some large school districts exercise considerable power as purchasing units, while others rely heavily upon suppliers for advice, thereby giving up the influence they might exercise on prices and the quality of the output. A recent estimate placed the purchases of supplies for public primary and secondary schools at $1.7 billion per year.

In many parts of the country, county governments have been squeezed because of the expansion of state and city governments; in other areas, they have expanded in response to new needs engendered by suburban development. Many county governments are involved in the operation of a variety of important enterprises such as hospitals, welfare homes, and community colleges. In most instances these governmental enterprises compete directly or indirectly with private and nonprofit enterprises. Some counties have recently expanded their own institutions after finding that it is less expensive to care for the indigent aged and chronically ill under their own supervision than to continue to cover the charges levied by private nursing homes or nonprofit institutions.

The St. Lawrence Seaway Development Corporation, which is the American counterpart of Canada's St. Lawrence Seaway Authority, is an illustration of joint action of two national governments. In cooperation with other agencies in each country, these two principal organizations planned, constructed, and now operate the navigation portion of the total project. The power development aspect of the larger program has been left to a state and a provincial agency, the Power Authority of New York State and the Hydro-Electric Power Commission of Ontario.

Cooperative action at the state level is represented by the Delaware River Port Authority established jointly by New Jersey and Pennsylvania and by the Port of New York Authority established jointly by New York and New Jersey. The establishment of these interstate enterprises requires both an act of incorporation by each state legislature and approval by Congress. Given the mission to improve the port and the transportation systems feeding it, the Port of New York Authority has built and leased or operated bridges, tunnels, piers, terminals for buses, truck and freight terminals, and airports in both states. It purchases and leases railroad cars to commuter railroads. It owns a number of industrial and marine properties. In each of its operations, it serves directly a wide variety of transportation companies as well as a host of subsidiary and related business enterprises, including hotels, restaurants, banks, and insurance companies.

Another instance of interstate governmental enterprise is the Southern Regional Educational Conference, established by a compact among the governors of thirteen Southern states in order to avoid duplication of expensive higher education facilities. The agreement provided that selected state institutions would concentrate in different fields and thereafter serve all the residents of the several states in the region. The Conference provides a mechanism for determining which schools will offer specific programs and permits students to pursue a specific educational program not offered in their home state. Students pay the same tuition to the out-of-state university as they would pay in their own state. The Western States Higher Educational Conference is a similar organization, with a looser organizational base.

Counties have joined together, with state approval, to form new government enterprises. These associations are usually concerned with transportation, recreation, water supply, and electric power. The San Francisco Bay Rapid Transit District at present has jurisdiction in four counties, and four other counties may opt to join later.

Cooperative action by cities, towns, and townships in the same metropolitan area is frequently necessary if important community needs are to be effectively met. New government enterprises can be established in a metropolitan area either by a compact among the political jurisdictions involved or by the creation of a special district. Both require state authorization. The state of Washington authorized Seattle and its surrounding suburbs to organize a multipurpose Municipality of Metropolitan Seattle, but the suburban electorate did not approve the measure. However, the Seattle–Lake Washington area voted to establish a pollution control district in 1958.

Similarly, the Boston Metropolitan Transit Authority serves the cities and towns in the greater Boston area.

Conventional governmental units are frequently inhibited by legal, administrative, or economic considerations from providing desired public services. To overcome these barriers, special districts are often established. For the most part, these special districts are concerned with providing a specific service and therefore tend to be single purpose enterprises, such as units involved in water and sewage, fire protection, sanitation, housing.

Joint action by governments at different levels may also call forth new enterprises or the expansion of existing ones. The Federal government recently secured congressional approval for its participation on a partnership basis with Delaware, New Jersey, New York, and Pennsylvania in the Delaware River Basin water resource development program. This is the first Federal-interstate compact enterprise. Another example is the venture of the Department of the Interior and the state of California, which are jointly engaged in the Central Valley project to divert water from the north to the arid south.

A very important stimulant for the creation of new enterprises, as well as for the expansion of existing activities, is the program of Federal grants-in-aid to the states. These have played a major role in stimulating state highway construction, vocational education, public works, welfare measures, and public health. Federal grants-in-aid are also available to state and interstate agencies for programs aimed at the control of water pollution, planning studies for the disposal of industrial waste, and the construction of waste disposal plants.

The Hill-Burton Act which was passed in 1946 made it possible for Federal funds to be given to the states for the construction or remodeling of state, local, and nonprofit hospitals and other medical facilities. The act also provides strong incentives for each state to appraise its existing hospital and public health center resources and to develop comprehensive state and local hospital and health facility construction plans.

A considerable part of the Federal grants to states is passed on to local units. In addition, some Federal grants are made directly to local units for urban renewal, low-cost public housing, airport construction, and waste disposal. These grants stimulate activities which might not be undertaken at all or only belatedly if revenues from the state and locality were the only sources of financing. Federal grants-in-aid programs also impose standards of performance. They represent a major reinforcement of our Federal-state system, since they encourage local initiative and local operating responsibility. In the absence of responses by state and local governments, the Federal government might be forced to assume a much more direct role in providing urgently needed services. The grant-in-aid approach also has the additional advantage of enabling Congress to apportion its expenditures with respect to differentials of need among the states and differentials in their ability to meet these needs from their own resources.

The states are an important source of funds to counties, municipalities, special districts, and school districts. Through grants for specific purposes, the states call forth matching funds from local agencies and in the process are able to set minimum standards of performance. The chief functions for which the states make payments to local governments are education, highways, welfare, health, and hospitals. Once again, these state grants-in-aid facilitate a substantial equalization of expenditures among the several subdivisions of the states.

An example of joint action by a city and a county was the creation of the Miami–Dade County government in Florida. Through a federation of the city and county, a revitalized county government has been created with additional functions and with the resources available to provide them.

We have seen that many new enterprise units were created through the joint efforts of governmental bodies. Others have been created through new relationships between government and private enterprise and nonprofit institutions. Whether a new enterprise is actually created or an existing one is modified, the impact of government is frequently substantial. Many private firms depend upon government contracts for most or all of their sales. An extreme case was the Martin Aircraft Company, which in 1958 sold 99.2 percent of its total output to the Federal government. Firms which rely upon government contracts for an overwhelming share of their business differ from conventional private enterprise almost as much as private enterprise differs from nonprofit or government enterprise.

Many government contractors begin operations at the behest of government, obtain construction and operating funds from government, secure access to raw materials or secret processes through government, limit their production largely to government orders, and manage their affairs in line with government suggestions. These "private" companies nevertheless are faced with major uncertainties about whether they will obtain new contracts and, in some cases, whether their "profits" are subsequently renegotiated. Firms which serve as subcontractors to government contractors may suffer even greater uncertainty about the renewal of contracts, changes in technology, the invasion of competing subcontractors, and an inability to predict their costs accurately.

The cold war and the rapid advances in science and military technology have enormously increased the Federal government's contracts for research and development. R & D contracts go to universities, to nonprofit laboratories and research organizations, and to private firms. The Defense Department, Atomic Energy Commission, NASA, and other government agencies have extensive contracts with private companies for the development and production of aircraft, missiles, rockets, electronics, equipment, and atomic energy for military and related uses.

Since these large public investments have for the most part been expended in order to perfect military and space technology, the Federal government has begun to offer direct and indirect support to various enterprises in the hope and expectation of finding commercial uses for some of the new technology. This support has been concentrated on the development of nuclear power and improvements in communications. At all levels of government, and especially at the Federal level, there has been a great expansion of programs to aid universities and nonprofit associations, and on occasion even profit-making enterprises, which are engaged in research in the field of science, medicine, education, social welfare, and other fields of direct interest and concern to the civilian sector. Governmental assistance has also involved support for the construction and expansion of research facilities as well as for the development of pilot programs in which the results of the research are tested.

In addition to the new patterns of relationship among government, nonprofit, and profit organizations that have grown out of the rapid expansion of R & D under the principle of governmental financing and nongovernmental performance, certain entirely new types of enterprise structures have emerged. The Rand Corporation, a nonprofit agency specifically organized to undertake research for the Air Force, provides a broad spectrum of analytical services on contract to the Air Force and to a lesser extent to other agencies. Similar groups established on a nonprofit basis are the Mitre Corporation, Institute for Defense Analyses, Systems Development Corporation, and Aerospace Corporation. As these names suggest, they are overwhelmingly involved in work for the defense and space agencies. Lockheed Missiles and Space Company, Boeing Aerospace Division, and Bendix Radio Division operate in much the same area, but these organizations are part of larger companies that operate to make profits.

The universities have utilized Federal funds for basic research, particularly in the physical and life sciences and in engineering, both by establishing new projects within the existing university departments and by establishing off-campus organizations to meet specific objectives. Among the latter are the Lincoln Laboratory, formerly of M.I.T., the Hudson Laboratories of Columbia University, the Jet Propulsion Laboratory under control of the California Institute of Technology, and the Institute of Science and Technology of the University of Michigan.

The significance of this new flow of Federal funds is suggested by the fact that grants from the National Institutes of Health and other Federal agencies to medical schools account for approximately one-fourth of their operating budgets. Further, the physical science departments and particularly the departments of physics at the nation's leading universities receive an overwhelming part of their total annual income from these governmental grants and contracts.

New enterprise forms and relationships have also developed as a consequence of attempts to utilize the results of atomic energy programs for the civilian economy. These attempts have given rise to problems with regard to the terms on which private industry should be allowed or encouraged to enter this field. Intertwined with the ongoing debate about the amount of Federal subsidy required to speed the development of nuclear power are hoary issues about the appropriate roles of private and public enterprise in the industry. Private companies seeking to produce atomic power have been selected by the Atomic Energy Commission from among competing applicants. The companies utilize the knowledge developed by the AEC through its research on reactors and fuels; they may work for the AEC on new research and development contracts, or they may turn to the AEC for help in solving some of their research problems. This cooperative relationship is made essential by the fact that the law for some years prevented the private ownership of atomic fuel. As a consequence, the uranium and thorium were supplied to the companies as needed, at prices far below their original cost to the government in order to encourage private experimentation. The AEC also exerts regulatory powers over the private companies for reasons of security and safety.

These are some of the many reasons for the close cooperative relationships between government and the private companies in this field. Time is constantly changing the elements
in this relationship, so that now there is not one pattern but a
great many different arrangements between the Federal government and the private companies. Despite the willingness
of the Federal and, more recently, state governments to be
helpful, some private companies such as Consolidated Edi-
son of New York City moved into the field of nuclear power
with the determination to go it alone just as far as possible. It
was willing to forego valuable types of governmental assistance in order to retain maximum freedom from governmental constraints.

The opportunity to utilize earth satellites for the purpose
of improving international and domestic communications
was met in a quite different way. The Communications
Satellite Corporation is a privately owned, federally char-
tered and supervised corporation. Three of the fifteen members of the Board of Directors are appointed by the President
of the United States. The corporation has sole right to own,
operate, and develop the United States' share in satellite communications for the relaying of messages by telephone, tele-
graph, and television. The launching of the satellite, however, is left to the government space agency. Here again,
technological considerations, in which foreign policy and defense issues are heavily involved, have resulted in a new pattern of enterprise requiring active cooperation between the
private sector and the Federal government.

We have noted that government enterprises frequently
produce services which private enterprise or nonprofit organizations also offer, either as a counterpart, supplement, or

competitor. The government and nonprofit sectors in particular overlap in providing certain functions, chiefly health,
education, and welfare services. In some fields, such as education, both sectors have continued to expand their facilities
in response to increases in demand. Both public and nonprofit schools exist side by side, that is, in both a competitive
and a complementary relationship. In other areas, such as
basic welfare programs, the establishment of government
services led to a withdrawal of nonprofit agencies from the
field.

Until the advent of the New Deal, private philanthropy
carried the principal responsibility for feeding and clothing
the unemployed. But the blistering Depression of the early
1930s created more need than even their expanded resources
could cope with. Government had to assume responsibility
for the millions of unemployed and their families. Slowly,
philanthropic agencies withdrew from what had been their
primary domain—the feeding and clothing of the poor.
These organizations then began to look for other types of
services that they might provide for the needy or those with
limited incomes. Many of them entered the field of family
counseling.

Government has given substantial stimulus to new enterprises in the nonprofit sector. The building of dormitories
and research facilities, the support of basic and applied research, and the financing of student education at colleges,
universities, medical schools, and schools of nursing are
aided through the National Institutes of Health, the National Science Foundation, and other government agencies.
Nonprofit hospitals have been built as a result of grants and
loans from the Hill-Burton funds. Cities and towns and

counties frequently provide facilities free or below cost for a municipal opera company or symphony orchestra. Many cooperative housing projects are dependent upon financial aid provided by government, while urban renewal projects depend on the government's power of eminent domain as well as government subsidies.

A recent striking innovation involving nonprofit enterprise and government is the creation of the nonprofit North Carolina Fund. It was established by the Governor of the state, a leading newspaper editor, a Negro banker, and an executive of one of the largest manufacturing companies in the state. The Fund's avowed purpose is to "develop the state's human resources to the fullest." Beginning with substantial grants from the Ford Foundation and other foundations, the Fund aims to raise matching sums from various levels of government. State and local agencies will administer the specific projects which range from improving methods of teaching in the first three grades to comprehensive community projects in selected urban and rural areas.

No effort has been made in the preceding review to indicate the scale of the economic activities carried on by the three major levels of government in the United States. These data will be presented later. We attempted instead to illuminate the diversity of the enterprise structures and the many innovations that have characterized this sector of the economy. The conventional view has been to consider innovation as restricted to the profit-seeking sector and the introduction of new products. But a realistic analysis of the dynamics of the economy indicates that innovation also has a role in the economic activities of the governmental and nonprofit sectors. And in an increasingly affluent society, innovation in the provision of new or better services may be as important as, or more important than, the innovation of new industrial or consumer products.

It may be useful to summarize the major forces that have contributed to a proliferation of government activities and particularly government enterprise structures. Considerable influence must be ascribed to the exploitation of new defense and space technology. This underlies much that is new in the economic activities of the Federal government.

Changing social values help to explain many new forms of government enterprise. The desire of the electorate to carry through many reforms can be implemented only by a government agency with powers of eminent domain as well as access to large capital resources. Existing government organizations at national, state, county, and local levels were found to be inadequate to meet the challenges of certain metropolitan and regional areas, with the result that new governmental structures were organized that were congruent with the underlying economic realities.

Since many state, county, and local governments operate under constitutional and other limitations as to the amount of indebtedness that they can incur and since these ceilings frequently put a limit on the electorate's ability to secure new or improved services, new governmental structures have been established free of these constraints. These new enterprises are able to enter the capital markets for funds at the same time that they are permitted and frequently encouraged to sell their products at a price that would cover all costs and even yield a surplus.

New government structures and relationships were developed to assure that in the pursuit of important public objectives optimal use was made of the strengths inherent in the profit and nonprofit sectors of the economy. A closely related reason was the belief that it was undesirable for government qua government to become increasingly involved in the direct production of goods and services.

The differential ability of various governmental units to meet urgent public needs or to increase the quantity and quality of existing public services led to new patterns of financial and administrative relationships among different levels of government.

Still another factor leading to new governmental structures has been the lack of willingness or ability of the private or nonprofit sector to respond adequately to urgent public needs. In addition, governments are sometimes under pressure to take over operations for which the private or nonprofit sectors are no longer able or willing to take responsibility. Often legislators, usually under public pressure for more efficient administration, seek to isolate large undertakings from political patronage by establishing quasi-independent structures with more scope for executive direction. Similarly, the electorate, desiring to pay only for what it uses, encourages the establishment of new structures where specific financing is easier to accomplish. In addition, since legislators are often faced with opposition from one or another section of the electorate, they may find it easier to secure approval for a specific program by devising a new structure through which to carry it out.

Finally, despite the profit-seeking orientation of the private sector there are many investments which it is loath to make, because the gains will be diffused rather than concentrated. It has therefore devolved upon government in recent decades to enlarge the community's investments in such fields as research, which in time have led to many new types of enterprise relationships.

The identification of these several forces helps to make two points clear. First, no one of them is entirely new. Each has operated in the past to condition the role of government in the economic life of the country. However, during the past three to four decades the United States has confronted serious challenges from within and without—depression, war, and cold war—and at the same time has confronted major new opportunities in education and human welfare. Second, as a result at many levels of government a great many innovations have been introduced. Governments responded both to the challenges and the opportunities.

However, as many new problems were raised as were solved. The public continues to be strongly divided about the proper role of government; the conflict might be designated as that of the proponents of larger expenditures versus those in favor of lower taxes. There is a division of opinion even about the drift of the last several decades, which have seen a substantial enlargement in the economic activities of government. This reflects the tolerance, in fact the approval, of the majority for these developments, but a significant minority continues to maintain a critical attitude.

Even within the consensus which has approved the broadening of government's enterprise role, there remains a divergence of opinion about the desirability of speeding or slowing the rate of its expansion. Moreover, there are differences about the areas into which government should move or where it should intensify its activities. Some lay primary stress on education, others on the urban environment, still others on the specialized needs of a particular population group, such as Negroes or the aged. The advocates of expansion agree only in principle. When it comes to details, conflicts continue.

Even if there were a meeting of the minds about the preferred fields for expanding government's activities, not all outstanding disagreements and conflicts would be dissolved, for the electorate does not even agree about the quality of services that government should provide. To favor the deeper involvement of government in the support of public education is one position, but it does not indicate the preferred level of effort. In some communities it might involve the establishment of a junior college; in others it may represent a commitment to spend additional public funds on the school system to assure that it remains among the strongest in the nation. Moreover, mere agreement that government activities should be expanded does not specify which level of government—Federal, state, local—should provide leadership. In many parts of the country the local electorate will move only if liberal Federal or state grants-in-aid are made available. In other places, the local group will tax itself if it is convinced that the new services are sufficiently important to warrant the additional burden.

Finally, there is considerable scope for differences of opinion, even among those who are in substantial agreement about the desirability of the expansion of government, about the preferred way of paying for the expansion. There is a wide range of options, from payment through regular tax sources, to borrowing inside or outside the established debt limits, to reliance on a system of fees or charges which will cover all or most of the costs of the additional services.

It is not easy to innovate in the field of government enterprise. Yet the record reveals that over the last several decades the United States has demonstrated a high degree of flexibility in devising new forms for expanding the government's role in the nation's economic life. The import and impact of these innovations still remain to be evaluated.

4

The Economic Activities
of Nonprofit Institutions

Now that we have expanded the conventional model of the
American economy to make provision for the large variety of
government enterprises, we must expand it further to make
room for the economic activities carried on by nonprofit institutions. What is the rationale for nonprofit institutions?
Cannot private enterprise or government do all that needs to
be done? The answer is close at hand. We need only mention the interest and concern of most Americans in having
the opportunity to pursue their religious activities. Clearly
these activities cannot be provided by a concern engaged in
the making of profits. But in this case neither can the government step in and provide this service. Under our constitutional prohibition against the involvement of government in
religion, neither the Federal, state, nor local governments can
build churches, pay the salaries of the clergy, and otherwise

provide the economic wherewithal for religious undertakings. Nonprofit institutions are essential to the effective functioning of a pluralistic society, and they have been an integral part of the American scene since the colonial period.

It is easy to see why religious activities must be conducted by organizations that are neither profit-seeking nor governmental. But how can we explain the great variety of nonprofit institutions? Many engage in activities of a charitable or eleemosynary nature which clearly fall outside the province of the profit-seeking sector. There is a tradition in Western civilization that is rooted in Judeo-Christian belief that the more fortunate should help to care for their less fortunate brothers. Many nonprofit institutions are rooted in this ethos, and colonial and later state legislatures were therefore willing to charter charitable organizations.

The long-standing, general disposition to restrict the growth of government reinforced the inclination of citizen-groups to join together on a voluntary basis to further important communal ends. There is a mutuality between a position which holds that government should not grow unless there is an absolute necessity and the position which sees many virtues in the voluntary association of citizens to accomplish important charitable and social objectives. At the turn of the century when an increasing number of very wealthy people adopted the practice of contributing very large sums to existing philanthropic institutions or to new ones which they established, a stimulus was provided to broaden and deepen the nonprofit sector. This was reinforced by the unwillingness of the majority of the electorate to have government assume responsibility for meeting new social needs or for meeting more adequately needs of long standing. An enlightened minority through voluntary effort set a new pattern and showed what money could accomplish. They hoped that in the process they could educate a sufficiently large group of previously disinterested citizens so that the government would eventually be permitted to assume broadened responsibilities. This pattern played a major role in the advance of health, educational, welfare, and recreational services.

Another force which operated in favor of the establishment and expansion of nonprofit organizations was the knowledge of possible gains that groups of farmers, laborers, employers, and others could achieve by banding together for the pursuit of a common economic or social objective. Nonprofit organizations were established to enable individual workers to participate in a pension fund, to enable farmers to market their products effectively, to enable employers to form a trade association which would broaden their access to trade information. If the aims and purposes of these organizations appeared to be in the public interest—and if they did not appear to injure any other group—they were likely to receive a state charter to pursue their objectives.

We see then that nonprofit organizations were established and nurtured because they provided an opportunity for different groups in the community to realize important goals which were not realizable under the aegis of profit-seeking or government organizations. In the pursuit of these goals they operate as enterprise units even though, as we will see, their market behavior can be distinguished in some regards from both profit-seeking organizations and government agencies.

In many ways, however, the economic operations of nonprofit organizations are indistinguishable from those of private profit-seeking enterprises. A secretary's job in the YMCA is as real as a secretary's job in General Motors. Workers are counted in the nation's employment statistics without reference to the legal form of the organization for which they work. Nonprofit organizations must offer approximately comparable conditions to those in private enterprise in order to attract and hold their clerical personnel, although they may compensate for somewhat lower salaries by additional nonpecuniary benefits.

A corporation which sells to both religious organizations and private companies treats the receipts from each purchaser identically, even if the terms of sale are not precisely the same. The investment market accepts money from union welfare and pension funds, endowments, and foundations on the same terms as those offered to individuals or corporations. A shopkeeper or landlord makes no distinction between money he receives from a wage earner and money given him by the recipient of charity from a nonprofit agency. When nonprofit organizations build housing or offer goods and services in the health, education, or recreation fields, they are in competition with private enterprise for the consumer's dollar. Contracts entered into by nonprofit agencies are enforceable in the courts in much the same way as are those of profit-seeking enterprises.

Nonprofit organizations provide a wide variety of services. The diversity is suggested by the following brief list of enterprises: the New York Stock Exchange, the Encyclopaedia Britannica, the Bronx Zoological Park, the New York Public Library. Many believe that one or more of these institutions is a government agency or a private business, but in point of fact each is a nonprofit institution.

However, nonprofit enterprises are heavily concentrated in three fields, whether their activities are measured in terms of numbers of employees or annual expenditures. The fields are education, health and hospital services, and religious activities.

Nonprofit enterprises contribute to total employment in several different ways. Most important is the direct employment of persons on their staffs. It is estimated that 3.3 million persons, or 4.9 percent of the labor force, were employed by nonprofit enterprises in 1960. The employees of nonprofit organizations are highly concentrated in professional and technical, clerical and service occupations. Hospitals, the largest source of nonprofit employment, accounted for an estimated total employment of 827,000 persons in 1960. Educational institutions, which range from primary school to graduate institutions, had 676,000 employees in professional and nonprofessional ranks. The nonprofit organizations such as mutual insurance companies, savings and loan associations, which operate much like private businesses, employed 843,000. Over 900,000 persons were employed by the thousands of other nonprofit institutions.

The effects on employment of nonprofit organizations extend far beyond the numbers on their own payrolls. In the first place, nonprofit agencies are a significant market for the sale of privately produced goods and services, and thus are indirectly responsible for the employment of many workers in the private sector. Secondly, the investments of savings and loan associations, of union pension and welfare funds, and of nonprofit foundation and university endowments stimulate employment in the private sector. Many governmental employees are engaged exclusively or primarily in providing services to such nonprofit organizations as farmers' cooperatives and savings and loan associations. Hence, their employment is indirectly dependent on these nonprofit institutions. There are a great many other government employees whose work consists of awarding and accounting for contracts and grants to universities, hospitals, and other nonprofit agencies.

If we were interested in the full ramifications of nonprofit organizations on employment, we would have to assess the unique role of nonprofit educational institutions in determining the output of trained personnel and the influence of trade unions on the operations of the labor market. In view of the strategic role that trained manpower has come to play in the continuing progress of the American economy and the strategic contribution that private universities make to the education and training of such high-level personnel, it would be hard to exaggerate the indirect effect of nonprofit institutions on the level of employment. It is the graduates of these nonprofit organizations who play a major role in basic research, the development of technology, and the provision of professional and managerial services.

We can further appreciate the amount of economic activity conducted by nonprofit organizations by reviewing the sources of their income. They solicit funds and gifts in kind from private individuals, businesses, corporations, foundations, and government units. They are regularly allocated funds in the budgets of corporations, foundations, Community Chests, and governments. Frequently capital fund drives are instituted specifically on their behalf. They also realize income and capital gains from their own investments or endowments. Finally, they receive payment for services which they render.

Because of the wide range of services which they provide, the full scope and impact of the operations of nonprofit organizations is generally obscured. The scope and diversity of nonprofit activities are indicated by the fact that most larger communities have found it not only desirable but necessary to establish coordinating organizations to facilitate relationships not only among the various nonprofit agencies but between these agencies and governmental bodies.

The diversity characteristic of the nonprofit sector is illustrated by a directory of community services, both public and nonprofit, in Nassau County, New York, recently published by two nonprofit coordinating agencies. The Nassau County Index lists nearly 150 organizations under 13 major headings: community organizations, correctional services, counseling services, health services, hospitals, mental health services, nursing organizations, professional organizations, recreational facilities, services for special groups, and services for the aging. Since many organizations are engaged in multiple functions, they are cross-listed.

Some of the nonprofit organizations in Nassau County are exclusively fund-raising and grant-distributing agencies. The Hospital Council, on which most of the voluntary hospitals of the area have members and the county hospitals and medical societies have associate members, is charged with the responsibility "to study, plan and develop hospital and related health facilities for more effective coordination in the accomplishment of economy, efficiency and closer relationship with other related health and welfare agencies, and the promotion of broader public knowledge and understanding of hospital services, problems and needs." There is a Council of Churches, representing Protestant and Greek Orthodox churches, which is concerned with the assignment of chaplains to colleges and hospitals, court workers for family and children's courts, radio programs, an audio-visual lending library, an annual clothing drive for overseas relief, and related activities. Other church groups provide similar services.

One agency aids released prisoners, particularly young ones, in obtaining employment, and provides housing and counseling services to speed their rehabilitation. There is a home for the blind, a hearing and speech society, a legal aid society, a family service association, a committee on alcoholism, and a home-school for girls. There are several institutions of higher education and libraries, as well as specialized schools for handicapped children who receive special attention. A foundation carries on a program of research and education in the biological, medical, psychological, and sociological aspects of the employment of disabled persons and also provides facilities in which disabled persons can exercise and swim. Other groups include a planned parenthood center, a self-help group of divorced, widowed, separated, or never-married parents who must raise children in a one-parent family.

There are, of course, many different ways of classifying nonprofit organizations. Some are self-help, with a membership which is restricted to individuals pursuing similar or common ends. Some have members who donate their time to providing services at little or no cost to disadvantaged groups who otherwise would have no access to such services. Some organizations, run by a paid professional staff, serve a varied number of people, many or all of whom pay for the services which they receive. Still others, such as a nonprofit research laboratory, are financed almost exclusively through government contracts which cover all capital as well as operating costs.

Nonprofit organizations may provide goods or services to identifiable recipients, such as free books for hospital patients, or, in the case of research organizations, to the public at large. Some organizations are national; others regional; still others are local; the scope of their financing and services is likely to reflect these differences. The entire capital of the Ford Foundation came from members of the Ford family, but the foundation's operations are national and international in scope. Boys Town, Nebraska, is centered in a single locality, but its appeal for funds is nationwide, and the boys who are selected for training come from all parts of the country.

Some nonprofit organizations may work in unique fields; others may complement and on occasion even compete with government or private enterprise. A nonprofit organization may be large and use substantial capital, such as hospitals, laboratories, and schools; or it may be small and utilize only a modest amount of labor and resources, such as a family counseling agency. Some train their own staff; others rely primarily on volunteers; still others bid trained labor away from other sectors. Some are expanding; others are static.

Some nonprofit organizations are little more than the "hobby-horse" of a wealthy donor or donors whose activities have little or no social or economic impact on the community. Others play a strategic role in the nation's life, such as the leading private universities. In every case they are dependent to some degree on the goodwill of government; some are completely dependent on government.

There is considerable variation in the legal status of non-profit organizations. Today nonprofit organizations are formed almost entirely by incorporation under various state laws which determine the organization's legal position. The laws of New York State, which legal experts adjudge to be the most comprehensive, indicate again the great diversity in the nonprofit sector. Under New York's general incorporation law nonprofit organizations, associations, clubs, and societies for social, athletic, political, civic, and charitable purposes may be formed. This law also permits other types of nonprofit organizations to be incorporated: cemeteries, volunteer fire departments, societies for cruelty prevention, Christian associations, medical societies, agricultural and horticultural fair societies, and boards of trade. In addition, there are special laws for other types of nonprofit associations. The law governing religious corporations has detailed provisions for the incorporation of twenty different types of denominational churches and cemeteries. The statutes governing education provide for the incorporation of educational, cultural, and professional institutions and societies. Agricultural cooperatives operate under a special law, as do farmers' and marketing associations, benevolent orders, and fraternal lodges. The statutes governing insurance regulate certain aspects of mutual organizations—financial, medical, and other. The statutes dealing with banks also cover credit unions and savings and loan associations. Miscellaneous statutes cover the incorporation and regulation of such special nonprofit organizations as horse-breeding and racing associations, hunt meetings, and other special types of organizations.

Indiana, in addition to a general incorporation act for nonprofit organizations, has almost thirty additional statutes governing the incorporation of particular types of nonprofit organizations. Indiana's special laws cover such fields as foundations and holding companies, coliseum building, poultry, dog and cat breeding, camp meeting associations, and missions. Michigan has a special statute for trade and labor associations. In the United States Internal Revenue Code, organizations are recognized as nonprofit if their activities are limited to one or more of a wide variety of purposes: charitable, educational, civic, religious, scientific, trade union, agricultural, horticultural, the prevention of cruelty to children and animals, social clubs, fraternal and employee beneficiary societies, business leagues, chambers of commerce, real estate boards, boards of trade, and cemetery associations.

The legal distinctions which the several states make about whether an association is nonprofit affect its organization and operation, its rights and privileges, and particularly its tax status. Federal regulations, particularly those dealing with tax matters, add further complexity. The Internal Revenue Code recognizes the above sixteen broad types of tax-exempt organizations, but each organization must apply individually for exemption. Moreover, tax exemption does not cover income derived from ancillary activities and the assumption of new activities, or a change in the mode of operating may result in the loss of tax exemption. For example, under the revised Treasury regulations of 1959, tax exemption is denied an otherwise qualified organization if it participates in any political campaign on behalf of any candidate for office or if it pursues any activities or objectives which may characterize it as an "action organization." In one instance an organization was ruled ineligible for tax exemption because it ran bingo games for a profit out of which it gave gifts of money to physicians who performed "free services" at city-operated baby clinics. Even organizations which are essentially charitable are not automatically granted tax exemption. On the other hand, because of the looseness of the law, foundations which operate primarily as a device for transforming corporate profits into capital gains in order to avoid paying corporate taxes are sometimes able to qualify as nonprofit organizations.

A series of congressional hearings over the past several years has had as its primary aim the revision of the law so that the business-like activities of nonprofit organizations will no longer be tax-exempt. The United States Treasury agrees with much of the criticism that has been levied against the present law and administrative practices, but it has been unable, at least in the opinion of the Congress, to design specific measures that will not make the cure worse than the disease. The difficulty of drafting effective rules and regulations to eliminate the business-like activities of nonprofit organizations has led some students to advocate a radical restriction on their freedom of action, including the recommendation that every foundation liquidate its assets within a relatively short period, perhaps within twenty-five years of its establishment.

The Federal tax system as it currently operates contributes to swelling the income of nonprofit organizations by reducing the taxable income of donors who make contributions of cash or property, thereby narrowing the "net cost" of giving money away. When rates on individual income went up to 91 percent, the net cost of large charitable gifts to those in the high income bracket was very low indeed. Prof. William Vickrey of Columbia University calculated a few years ago that of the $3 billion or so donated to religious organizations, the tax savings constituted $900 million. That is, if taxpayers had not made deductible contributions to churches, they would have had to pay an additional $900 million in taxes. Even at today's much lower maximum rates, the tax subsidy for philanthropic contributions remains substantial.

Current Treasury rulings allow as deductible from gross income for tax purposes only contributions to nonprofit organizations or special subdivisions of them, organized and operated exclusively for religious, charitable, scientific, literary, or educational purposes or for the prevention of cruelty to children or animals; to domestic fraternal societies organized on the lodge system, provided the contributions are used only for eleemosynary purposes; to war veterans' organizations; and to cemetery companies or associations with no profit-seeking activities. Some organizations are exempt from paying Federal taxes, but contributions to them cannot be claimed as a deduction from taxable income. Among these are civic organizations, social clubs, boards of trade, chambers of commerce, labor organizations, and political parties.

Without any doubt, exemption from liability to taxation represents the most valuable right of nonprofit organizations. But they have other important advantages that facilitate their operations. Many nonprofit organizations are exempt from the Fair Labor Standards Act and the unemployment compensation laws. Participation in the social security program is optional for some tax-exempt organizations, which also receive special treatment with respect to the taxation of their annuity programs. Federal statutes provide that under certain circumstances nonprofit organizations may be exempted from admissions taxes, taxes on dues and initiations, manufacturers' and retailers' excise taxes, transportation and communication taxes, and documentary stamp taxes. Other Federal benefits which accrue to certain nonprofit organizations are the rights to acquire surplus property and preferential postal rates. All these benefits pertain only to nonprofit organizations; none are available to profit-seeking enterprises.

Most nonprofit organizations, of course, are eager to take full advantage of the tax exemptions for which they are eligible. Some years ago Butler University in Indiana created a stir when it renounced its right to tax exemptions on commercial, industrial, and residential property which it owned, because these exemptions were depriving local government of its principal source of revenue—real estate taxes. In communities where religious or educational institutions own a large amount of land, the municipality may be unable to raise adequate revenues if they rely primarily on the taxation of real estate.

Nonprofit organizations tend to shift the focus and nature of their operations in response to changing conditions in their environment. We noted earlier that some nonprofit enterprises have come to operate in much the same way as profit-seeking corporations. This is true particularly of mutual insurance companies, savings and loan associations, and cooperatives. Other nonprofit institutions have altered the nature of services they offer; many museums in the United States have been transformed from mere storehouses into educational institutions. Today many millions attend courses, lectures, concerts, dance recitals, and theatrical performances presented under the auspices of the revitalized museums. Officials of the nonprofit American Association of Museums recently discussed their new responsibilities toward the public—responsibilities which, they believe, include the need to coordinate museums with schools, colleges, and industry.

A similar radical expansion or transformation has occurred in other areas. The American Medical Association announced some time ago that it was establishing a center for registering adverse reactions to drugs. Local, state, and national medical societies are increasingly involved in sponsoring educational activities so that their members can keep abreast of new developments in medicine and related disciplines. The Philadelphia Mental Health Clinic greatly expanded its clientele when it instituted a round-the-clock "dial-a-psychiatrist" service which puts distressed individuals immediately in touch with a psychiatrist.

A basic rationale for nonprofit organizations is society's need for enterprises that are willing to experiment and lead the way in areas which cannot attract profit-seeking businessmen and where governments cannot enter. Many nonprofit organizations have fulfilled the task of serving on society's cutting edge in many crucial fields including health, education, and welfare.

But there is another side to the story. Many nonprofit organizations, particularly foundations, proceed with excessive caution, so that instead of leading the way they are frequently followers, putting their money where others have proved that a reasonable social return can be anticipated. Even more disturbing is the fact that well-endowed nonprofit organizations are likely to continue in their accustomed ways long after conditions have changed and the need for their services has diminished. This has happened with many well-endowed convalescent homes, tuberculosis sanatoriums, child welfare institutions, and homes for crippled children. A board with sentimental ties to a founder or a cause, reinforced by strong financial resources, and lulled by an unimaginative bureaucracy, may be substantially immune to pressures to change.

However, the forces of change in a dynamic society have led many other nonprofit organizations to reconsider their objectives and their methods. Many have shifted the focus of their work even to the extent of entering completely new fields of social endeavor. Moreover, in many instances the respective roles of business, nonprofit, and government enterprises in meeting various community needs have undergone radical shifts. Today private nursing homes play a major role in caring for the aged who are chronically ill. Government, through social security and public assistance, has assumed much of the responsibility for financing this effort. Nevertheless, voluntary organizations continue to play a role, particularly when it comes to securing capital funds for erecting or expanding the homes which they operate.

The expanded influence of government can also be found in the more aggressive role that it has begun to play in the formulation of basic standards and their enforcement. While the best of the nonprofit agencies are likely to operate at levels far above approved minimum standards, there are a great many institutions in the fields of health, education, and welfare where government authorities must be continuously vigilant to assure prevailing standards.

Important changes have also taken place in the manner in which nonprofit organizations are financed. Except in the case of religious organizations, reliance was placed in the past almost exclusively upon wealthy donors or patrons. But the rise of a substantial middle class, high income tax rates, and new methods of collecting funds have substantially altered the patterns of support. While small numbers of large givers still play a dominant role in most philanthropic undertakings, a broadened base of support now characterizes many nonprofit undertakings. A striking case has been the rapid increases in community fund drives which allocate the money they raise to a wide range of cooperating organizations.

As suggested earlier, the various levels of government have also come to play a much more important role in providing the operating funds—and some capital assistance—to many nonprofit institutions. In certain instances, such as institutions for the care of children and the aged, almost all the operating funds are governmental; in other cases the financial contribution of government is substantial.

But nonprofit institutions have sought other sources of funds. The most striking development has been the institution of charges for their services. This has been particularly true in voluntary general hospitals which today receive about 96 percent of their operating income from payments by and on behalf of patients.

While differences between profit and nonprofit enterprises are narrowing with respect to charging consumers for the services, important distinctions remain. While nonprofit enterprises obtain capital from various sources, they need not contemplate paying dividends, although mutual financial institutions and cooperatives divide their earnings among their members as a distribution of "savings." And many donors make gifts to universities for specialized research or the training of students in certain professions in the expectation of some return—in the hope that the donor firm or industry will benefit from the flow of new knowledge and trained manpower. But the direct financial return anticipated by an investor in a private enterprise is not expected by donors to a nonprofit organization.

Significant differences exist between profit and nonprofit organizations with respect to their management structures and the manner in which executives operate. In small voluntary organizations the key group is frequently composed of men and women who devote considerable time and energy to directing the operation on a part-time basis without any recompense other than the satisfaction they gain from participating and the social status and prestige that are usually attached to these positions. The routine operations are usually in the hands of a paid professional staff. Since these voluntary organizations are not directly under competitive market pressures, it is frequently difficult to assess the competence of the paid staff. Moreover, there is often room for favoritism and nepotism because of the direct role played by one or more of the board members who provide a substantial part of the financing.

In large nonprofit organizations the professional staff is likely to have considerable scope for action, but even here, as in large voluntary hospitals and family and child welfare organizations, the board may be directly involved in all decisions of importance. On the other hand, in private colleges and universities, the administration and the faculty have much greater scope for determining day-to-day operations and for introducing changes into the curriculum. Finally, in "nonprofit businesses," such as mutual savings banks and life insurance companies, the paid management is largely in control: the board of directors is involved only in broad policy issues and in the selection of new management. Even in these matters the board is likely to be influenced by the recommendations put forth by the existing management, particularly if it has proved to be competent.

The wide diversity of nonprofit organizations makes it impossible to put forth any simple generalizations about their management or to establish a clear basis for contrasting it with the structure and role of management of profit-seeking enterprises which also vary from small, closely held family enterprises to mammoth corporations. Nevertheless, a few gross distinctions may be ventured with regard to the forces which help to allocate management talent between the profit and nonprofit sectors and the rewards which each is likely to receive.

For a long time, the salaries earned by the heads of even the largest nonprofit organizations were considerably below those paid to men with comparable responsibility in business. In recent years, the boards of directors of some of the large nonprofit organizations have realized that to attract and hold managerial and professional talent requires that they offer salaries that begin to approximate those prevailing in private industry. Even these organizations are likely to pay a senior executive a lower monetary salary, but they may provide him with valuable fringes such as a house, an automobile, a chauffeur, and even significant entertainment allowances. As a nonprofit organization grows, it faces greater pressures to compete in the marketplace for scarce resources including managerial personnel.

Services produced by many nonprofit organizations, similar to those produced by many government enterprises, are "public goods" and are not consumed directly by individuals, as usually happens with the output of private enterprises. The individuals who receive specific services from a nonprofit child welfare agency, for example, are frequently identifiable, but in other instances it is diffuse contribution to the community which dominates. This characterizes the nonprofit organization that devotes its activities to the maintenance of a museum or the upkeep of a public recreational area. At the opposite extreme it may be difficult to differentiate the activities of certain nonprofit organizations from private enterprises. A case in point is the narrow line that separates certain nonprofit research laboratories from their profit-seeking counterparts.

Despite these parallels there are some important differences between profit-seeking and nonprofit enterprises with regard to their pricing policies. Although services which the public purchases from nonprofit organizations may be priced differently for different classes of customers, it is still possible that none of the prices bears close relation to actual costs. For instance, admission prices to nonprofit concerts or opera performances may vary according to the seat locations, but still receipts may not cover costs. A comparable private venture will fail if it cannot cover costs, since it cannot carry on a fund-raising campaign among the public.

As a matter of public policy, Blue Cross long had identical

rates for all groups in the community. However, private insurance companies charge more for older people, fathers of large families, and applicants with a history of illness. Recently the competition of private companies has forced many Blue Cross plans to introduce specific rates for different classes of subscribers.

Since the aim of philanthropy is to make useful goods and services available to the poor who could not otherwise secure them, many nonprofit organizations long followed the practice of offering their services free of charge or at a price far below cost. As a consequence, their pricing policy was frequently so haphazard that it did not even justify the term "policy." Recently, however, several forces have been operating to alter the situation and to force many nonprofit organizations to rationalize their pricing structure. Many middle- and even high-income groups increasingly desire to obtain the services of nonprofit organizations, such as universities, hospitals, symphony orchestras. However, philanthropy has not been able to provide subsidized services for all. Moreover, there is no reason why wealthy persons should give large sums away so that others in the middle-income brackets can obtain services free of charge or substantially below cost.

The transition from the old to the new approach to pricing has left many anomalies. Room rates for private patients in many nonprofit hospitals still cover only current expenses; in these hospitals wealthy patients may continue to receive a subsidy with respect to the capital costs of hospital care.

Many hospitals, colleges, and other nonprofit institutions continue to price their services at or below cost, and some continue to provide services to certain groups without charge. Nonprofit agencies have a personal approach and a welfare orientation which is lacking in profit-seeking enterprises. They are often overtly discriminatory, such as when they make special efforts to attract those who cannot pay their regular rates. This is true of colleges which offer scholarships to deserving students.

The process of costing is not the same in profit-seeking and nonprofit enterprises. The latter are only slowly coming to consider cost accounting systems, which charge interest on invested capital and depreciation on plant and equipment. Because these expenses are so often neglected in computing costs, tuition at nonprofit colleges and the charges made by many hospitals bear even less relation to true costs than the public generally assumes to be the case. If we consider the savings in taxes enjoyed by nonprofit institutions, the pricing of their services customarily contains a further element of subsidy to the typical consumer.

The enlarged scale of financial operations characteristic of such nonprofit enterprises as universities and hospitals and the further fact that many of their services are now paid for by insurance or by government have created a powerful stimulus for strengthening their cost accounting procedures. Universities have found that there are important overhead costs connected with their acceptance of research grants, such as the utilization of scarce space, library and laboratory facilities, the processing of personnel records, and other aspects involved in their expansion of staff. Since many government agencies have substantial research and development monies to allocate, the universities have attempted to develop a realistic set of accounts in the hope that the Federal government will agree to pay full costs. After many years of wrangling this has recently come to be established practice in many, but not all, government agencies involved in the allocation of research money. Columbia University, which receives about $45 million annually in government contracts and grants, has calculated that about 23 percent of total costs is overhead, which is now covered in most government contracts. Hospitals pursuing research programs supported by outside grants and contracts have begun to require that the funding cover overhead. The question is beginning to emerge of including capital costs in the hospital rates which form the basis of Blue Cross and commercial insurance reimbursement. However, many institutions are moving cautiously since they recognize that they may stand to gain on balance if they continue to pursue their long-term practices of looking to the community for their capital funds, including funds required for replacement and modernization.

The activities of many nonprofit institutions are directly linked to the operations of private enterprise. Important research, educational, and informational activities are carried on both by nonprofit organizations established, controlled, and financed by profit-seeking enterprises and by nonprofit institutions of independent character, such as universities and research institutions. Recently C.I.T. Financial Corporation, a profit-seeking enterprise, announced a "pay-as-you-go" plan for colleges and preparatory schools which lack the requisite funds, but desire to construct dormitories. Another example is the approach followed in New York City and in certain other localities whereby private enterprises, especially savings banks engaged in renovating slum properties in association with a nonprofit foundation, seek to assure the underwriters a reasonable yield of 8 to 10 percent instead of the typically exorbitant gains made by the owners of certain slum properties. Another example is the United Student Aid Funds, a nonprofit organization, which has persuaded commercial banks in many states to make low-interest loans at cost to college and university students by guaranteeing the loans. To be eligible for these loans, the students must also obtain financial assistance from the college and must demonstrate need and an inability to obtain loans from conventional commercial sources.

This summary review points up the great range of nonprofit institutions in our economy and their important role in enabling our society to realize its objectives and goals.

The impact of these activities on the private sector of the economy, as well as on the economy as a whole, has, on occasion, fundamental significance. Existing industries may be made obsolescent and new industries established as a result of major breakthroughs in research in nonprofit institutions. In the latter instance the flow of capital will be affected. The introduction of new products and processes will leave its mark on consumer preferences and their expenditure patterns. The laboratories of leading nonprofit organizations, particularly universities, represent a major dynamic center of the contemporary economy.

The influence and impact of changes also work in the opposite direction. Changes in the private enterprise sector are helping to transform the nature of nonprofit institutions. Marked changes are under way in the structure and functioning of many nonprofit institutions, particularly as more and more begin to shift their reliance from large-scale philanthropic gifts to the sale of services. Perhaps the most important conclusion to be derived from the foregoing analysis is that the nonprofit sector and the government and business sectors are becoming so interdependent that the differences among them are frequently more legal than economic. Many nonprofit organizations are directly involved in the production of services that are basic to the successful operation of both the profit sector and government; and in many instances they operate very much like private enterprises except for the advantages that accrue to them from tax exemption which they usually return to the public by establishing a lower price scale.

One unequivocal conclusion emerges: A complete description of the American economy requires the inclusion of the nonprofit sector.

5

The Scale and Scope
of the Not-for-Profit Sector

One consequence of the long-time concern of economists and businessmen with the central role of private profit-seeking enterprises in the operation of the American economy has been that the specialists in national income accounting have devoted inadequate attention to the economic contribution of the government and nonprofit sectors, which together comprise the not-for-profit sector. Comprehensive data for this not-for-profit sector is therefore not available, and we are handicapped in an attempt to assess the scale and significance of the output contributed by government and nonprofit institutions to the national income. But sufficient information is available to permit us to venture a first approximation.

The growth of an economic sector can be described in terms of output, income, employment, and other measures.

In assessing the production of services, even more than in the case of goods, changes in output are difficult to measure because one crucial aspect of growth, improvements in quality, does not lend itself readily to statistical measurement. A 1965 Ford may differ greatly from a 1930 Ford, but each is counted as one automobile. If a condition requiring surgery (and often resulting in amputation or death) in 1930 can be successfully treated with drugs in 1965, how does one compare the two courses of treatment? In our analysis of the not-for-profit sector, we will therefore rely primarily on money measures with some explanation of the factors which lie behind the dollar magnitudes.

Whenever students seek to assess the significance of changes in any important segment of the economy over a period of time, they face the problem of taking into account price changes which reflect alterations in the value of money as well as those which reflect shifts in the market position of particular goods or services. There are no comprehensive data available that would enable us to take full account of the effect of alterations in the general price level on the output of goods and services provided by government or by nonprofit institutions. To get around this difficulty, we will seek to illuminate the changing role of the not-for-profit sector by relating its expenditures at various points in time to the gross national product.

We will start by tracing two types of expenditures: those made to pay the salaries of employees directly employed by government and nonprofit institutions and expenditures made by these two sectors to purchase goods and services from the private sector. We will rely on the basic data com-

Item	1929	1940	1950	1960	1963
Gross national product	$104,436	$100,618	$284,599	$502,601	$583,918
Not-for-profit sector, total	13,067	18,571	52,624	129,582	159,639
Compensation of employees	7,031	10,822	29,321	65,832	81,060
Purchases from profit sector	6,036	7,749	23,303	63,750	78,579
Governments, total	9,240	15,057	41,705	105,426	129,713
Compensation of employees	5,093	8,762	23,490	52,528	64,505
Purchases from profit sector	4,147	6,295	18,215	52,898	65,208
General government	8,482	14,073	39,029	100,196	123,387
Compensation of employees	4,335	7,778	20,814	47,298	58,179
Purchases from profit sector	4,147	6,295	18,215	52,898	65,208
Government businesses	758	984	2,676	5,230	6,326
Compensation of employees	758	984	2,676	5,230	6,326
Nonprofit sector, total	3,827	3,514	10,919	24,156	29,926
Compensation of employees	1,938	2,060	5,831	13,304	16,555
Purchases from profit sector	1,889	1,454	5,088	10,852	13,371
Nonprofit institutions	3,034	2,668	8,835	19,878	24,895
Compensation of employees	1,145	1,214	3,747	9,026	11,524
Purchases from profit sector	1,889	1,454	5,088	10,852	13,371
Nonprofit businesses	793	846	2,084	4,278	5,031
Compensation of employees	793	846	2,084	4,278	5,031

sources: U.S. Department of Commerce; Federal Reserve System; U.S. Office of Education; American Hospital Association.

piled by the Department of Commerce. This procedure will enable us to derive a series of cross-sectional views of the scale and scope of the not-for-profit sector of the economy at different points in time. This will give a basis for judging absolute and relative rates of growth of this sector.

Table 5.1 presents an overview of the changing scale and scope of the not-for-profit sector during the past three and a half decades, which were marked by such diverse forces as prosperity, depression, war, and cold war. The changing scale and significance of the not-for-profit sector are brought into further perspective by an inspection of Table 5.2, which presents the percentage of the total gross national product accounted for by the purchases of the sector and its major subcomponents.

A scanning of the tables indicates that marked changes in the scale of the not-for-profit sector did occur between 1929 and 1963. At the end of the New Era, in 1929, the sector accounted for 12.5 percent of all the goods and services purchased. A decade later the figure stood at 18.5 percent, and in 1963 it was slightly above the 27 percent mark. These few figures clearly indicate the importance of modifying our old-time model of the economy as primarily a reflection of the activities of private enterprise to take account of the scale and significance of the not-for-profit sector.

A few words of explanation about the categories into which the not-for-profit sector has been divided. Government has been divided between two types of activities: general government and government businesses. The latter include those agencies whose operating costs are covered in full or at least to a substantial extent by the sales of goods and services, such as the post office, public power systems, state

PERCENT OF GROSS NATIONAL PRODUCT, 1929–1963

Item	1929	1940	1950	1960	1963
Not-for-profit sector, total	12.5	18.5	18.5	25.8	27.3
Compensation of employees	6.7	10.7	10.3	13.1	13.9
Purchases from profit sector	5.8	7.8	8.2	12.7	13.4
Government, total	8.8	15.0	14.7	21.0	22.2
Compensation of employees	4.8	8.7	8.3	10.5	11.0
Purchases from profit sector	4.0	6.3	6.4	10.5	11.2
General government	8.1	14.0	13.7	19.9	21.1
Compensation of employees	4.1	7.7	7.3	9.4	9.9
Purchases from profit sector	4.0	6.3	6.4	10.5	11.2
Government businesses	0.7	1.0	0.9	1.1	1.1
Compensation of employees	0.7	1.0	0.9	1.1	1.1
Nonprofit sector, total	3.7	3.5	3.8	4.8	5.1
Compensation of employees	1.9	2.0	2.0	2.6	2.9
Purchases from profit sector	1.8	1.5	1.8	2.2	2.2
Nonprofit institutions	2.9	2.7	3.1	4.0	4.3
Compensation of employees	1.1	1.2	1.3	1.8	2.1
Purchases from profit sector	1.8	1.5	1.8	2.2	2.2
Nonprofit businesses	0.8	0.8	0.7	0.8	0.8
Compensation of employees	0.8	0.8	0.7	0.8	0.8

SOURCES: U.S. Department of Commerce; Federal Reserve System; U.S. Office of Education; American Hospital Association.

liquor stores, and municipal waterworks. General government includes all other government operations including those which provide their services free of charge as well as those whose fees and charges cover only a nominal part of their costs, such as veterans' hospitals and state universities.

The nonprofit sector is likewise divided into two segments: institutions and businesses. The former include nonprofit universities, colleges, schools, hospitals, religious organizations, social and athletic clubs, labor organizations, and charitable and welfare organizations. Nonprofit businesses include mutual financial institutions, producers' and consumers' cooperatives, trade associations, and the like.

If we consider only payments for goods and services, as in Table 5.2, we find that total direct and indirect government expenditures increased from 8.8 percent of gross national product in 1929 to over 22.2 percent in 1963. This means that of all the goods and services produced by the economy in 1963 more than one-fifth represents output produced or purchased by governmental units, involving transactions with individuals and the general public as well as with business enterprises.

Changes have also taken place in the economic activity of the nonprofit sector. Total expenditures of the nonprofit sector increased from $3.8 billion in 1929 to $29.9 billion in 1963 or from 3.7 percent to 5.1 percent of gross national product.

In 1929, the not-for-profit sector divided its expenditures almost equally between employee compensation and purchases from private enterprises. Although the data for selected intervening years show some variability, the pattern in 1963 was not substantially different from what it had been in 1929. Employee compensation by general government and nonprofit institutions—the largest segments of the not-for-profit sector—amounted in 1963 to about 12 percent of all expenditures of those sectors.

The fact that both government and nonprofit institutions spend about the same amount on purchases from the private sector as they do on hiring personnel indicates again that in assessing the scale and scope of the not-for-profit sector it is essential to consider its purchases from the private sector. When a government agency or a nonprofit institution buys appliances, equipment, or services from the private sector, it has a direct effect on the number of employees that the private sector hires as well as on the profitability of the private sector, the rate at which it consumes its capital, and its incentives to invest. Many a businessman knows that the government is his best customer, and he makes his plans accordingly.

The preceding tables do not reveal the full scope of governmental and nonprofit spending during this period. For instance, they do not include interest paid on national, state, or local debts. They do not include spending by government or nonprofit businesses for goods and services bought from the private sector which are subsequently resold. They do not include welfare or social security payments, pensions, money gifts, or grants to individuals by either governments or nonprofit institutions. Moreover, governmental grants and payments to nonprofit institutions which are used for their internal operations are included as part of the expenditures of these institutions, not as part of governmental expenditures. The scale of the excluded expenditures is suggested by Table 5.3, which indicates that over the period 1929 to 1963, governmental payments for welfare, social security, pensions, and grants increased from 0.9 to 5.9 percent of gross national product.

Table 5.3 GOVERNMENT PAYMENTS FOR SOCIAL SECURITY, WELFARE, PENSIONS, AND GIFTS AND GRANTS, 1929–1963

Item	1929	1940	1950	1960	1963
			(in millions)		
Total	$909	$2,683	$14,304	$27,287	$34,287
Federal government	691	1,421	10,884	22,242	28,287
State and local governments	218	1,262	3,420	5,045	6,000
		(as percent of gross national product)			
Total	0.9	2.7	5.0	5.4	5.9
Federal government	0.7	1.4	3.8	4.4	4.9
State and local governments	0.2	1.3	1.2	1.0	1.0

SOURCE: U.S. Department of Commerce.

Table 5.4 presents an overview of the changes that have taken place during the last three and a half decades in the significance of the not-for-profit sector in the compensation of all employees. In 1929 the sector accounted for about one-seventh of the national wage bill; in 1963 its share had risen to almost one quarter.

From the data presented up to this point, one unequivocal conclusion emerges. The not-for-profit sector plays a markedly larger role in the national economy today than in 1929. Most of the increase reflects the growth of government, but there has also been a substantial expansion in the nonprofit area.

We must now determine whether the principal forces underlying the substantial increase in the not-for-profit sector can be identified and appraised. A start can be made by reviewing the transformations that occurred in the economy as the gross national product increased from $104 billion in 1929 to $584 billion in 1963. Table 5.5 presents certain key data about these three and a half decades. Within the framework of rapid growth, which in this table is exaggerated since the figures have not been deflated for general changes in the price level, we find both significant elements of stability and important alterations in the several components of the economy. In the goods-producing sector, it appears as if there has been a slight downward drift if the terminal years are compared. However, in 1950—at a time when most of the shortages of goods resulting from World War II had been eliminated—the sector accounted for several more percentage points than it had in 1929. Nevertheless, the contribution of the service sector to gross national product has risen over these decades.

Table 5.4 COMPENSATION OF EMPLOYEES IN THE NOT-FOR-PROFIT SECTOR AS PERCENTAGE OF TOTAL, 1929–1963

Item	1929	1940	1950	1960	1963
Total national employee compensation (in millions)	$51,085	$52,129	$154,190	$293,648	$340,309
			(as percent of total)		
Not-for-profit sector, total	13.8	20.8	19.0	22.4	23.9
Governments, total	10.0	16.8	15.2	17.9	19.0
General government	8.5	14.9	13.5	16.1	17.1
Government business	1.5	1.9	1.7	1.8	1.9
Nonprofit sector, total	3.8	4.0	3.8	4.5	4.9
Nonprofit institutions	2.2	2.4	2.4	3.1	3.4
Nonprofit business	1.6	1.6	1.4	1.4	1.5

SOURCE: U.S. Department of Commerce.

Item	1929 Amount (in millions)	1929 Percent distribution	1950 Amount (in millions)	1950 Percent distribution	1960 Amount (in millions)	1960 Percent distribution	1963 Amount (in millions)	1963 Percent distribution
Gross national product	$104,436	100.0	$284,599	100.0	$502,601	100.0	$583,918	100.0
By type of product:								
Goods	56,300	53.9	163,618	57.5	257,100	51.2	290,200	49.7
Construction	11,200	10.7	31,216	11.0	56,700	11.2	65,200	11.2
Services	37,000	35.4	89,765	31.5	188,800	37.6	228,400	39.1
National Income	$ 87,814	100.0	$241,876	100.0	$414,497	100.0	$478,493	100.0
By industry:								
Agriculture, forestry, and fisheries	8,278	9.4	17,923	7.4	17,295	4.2	18,903	4.0
Mining	2,048	2.3	5,010	2.1	5,510	1.3	5,414	1.1
Contract construction	3,808	4.3	11,833	4.9	21,786	5.3	24,758	5.2
Manufacturing	21,888	24.9	74,371	30.7	121,025	29.1	137,369	28.7
Wholesale and retail trade	13,358	15.2	42,707	17.7	67,698	16.3	77,367	16.2
Finance, insurance, and real estate	12,693	14.5	21,789	9.0	42,586	10.3	48,712	10.2
Transportation	6,636	7.6	13,278	5.5	17,909	4.3	19,474	4.1
Communications and public utilities	2,864	3.3	7,198	3.0	16,808	4.1	19,325	4.0
Services	10,338	11.8	23,089	9.5	49,065	11.8	59,465	12.4
Government	5,093	5.8	23,490	9.7	52,528	12.7	64,505	13.5
Rest of world	810	0.9	1,188	0.5	2,287	0.6	3,196	0.7

SOURCE: U.S. Department of Commerce.

The data which reflect the contribution of the principal "industries" to national income reveal a little more. They point up the relative declines since 1929 in agriculture, mining, finance, insurance, real estate, and transportation. The expanding sectors since 1929 were government and manufacturing. The latter expanded greatly between 1929 and 1950, but has shown relatively little change since then.

There are strong reasons for concentrating our analysis on recent experience—1950 to 1963—not only because it is recent but because the earlier period was distorted so severely by depression and war. Yet we must recognize the dangers involved in treating any fourteen-year period as a base for projections. There is no guarantee that the forces characteristic of such a relatively short period will continue to operate in the years ahead. But with this caution in mind, a more careful look at developments since mid-century may prove suggestive if not definitive.

Two suggestive findings emerge: there was a pronounced relative shift from goods to services in the recent period. Moreover, the trends that characterized different industries in the recent period (1950 to 1963) were a continuation of early developments. For the most part industries that relatively expanded, remained stable, or declined prior to 1950 continued along the same path after 1950.

One additional comment may be relevant. The changes in the contributions of the different industries to the national income do not provide a clear explanation for the substantial changes in the not-for-profit sector itself. We must look further to explain the latter. The expenditure patterns of government may provide an important clue. Table 5.6 presents these data.

Table 5.6 PURCHASES OF GOODS AND SERVICES BY GENERAL GOVERNMENT, 1929–1963 *(in millions)*

Item	1929	1940	1950	1960	1963
Total	$8,482	$14,073	$39,029	$99,616	$122,559
Federal, total	1,311	6,170	19,348	53,184	64,666
National defense	} 1,344	2,223	14,257	45,687	55,198
Other	}	3,956	5,202	8,024	10,296
Less government sales*	33	9	111	580	828
State and local	7,171	7,903	19,681	46,485	57,893

*Includes sales of previously purchased goods.
SOURCE: U.S. Department of Commerce.

95

Several important deductions can be drawn from this table. In 1929, state and local governments made more than 84 percent of all government purchases of goods and services. The years of the Great Depression and its aftermath found only a modest rise in the purchases of state and local governments in comparison with a four and a half times increase in the purchases of the Federal government. By 1940 the Federal government accounted for about 44 percent of all government purchases. An almost threefold increase in total government purchases took place between 1940 and 1950 when the Federal government made almost half of all these expenditures. The last thirteen-year period has witnessed a further rapid growth in government expenditures, primarily by the Federal government. In 1964 it accounted for about 53 percent of total government purchases.

Other findings can be extracted from the table. In 1940 expenditures for national defense accounted for only slightly more than one-third of Federal purchases and only one-sixth of all government purchases. In 1963 national defense accounted for over 85 percent of all Federal purchases and not much less than half of all government purchases. There is no mystery about the single most important factor responsible for the growth of government expenditures. It is the national determination to build and maintain a strong defense position.

But while national defense explains much, it does not explain all. The same table reveals a very rapid increase in state and local purchases during the recent period, an increase from under $20 billion in 1950 to about $57 billion in 1963. These increases reflect the rapidly growing expenditures of state and local governments firstly for education and secondly for all of the other basic services which they must provide for a rapidly growing and increasingly urbanized population. The fact that state and local governments had been unable to make new investments between 1929 to 1945, first because of financial stringency and then because of the war, further helps to explain their recent spurt.

The rate of expenditures by government is conditioned by several variables: the presence of a major threat such as a war or severe depression; the desire of the citizenry and their ability to pay for expanded and improved services that are conventionally provided by government; the extent to which other sectors of the economy are able to meet part or all of the demand for such services. As we have noted, the rapid rise in the purchases of the Federal government during the 1930s was in response to the Great Depression; its more recent high level of expenditures reflects primarily the involvement of the United States in war and the threat of war.

The changing role of the not-for-profit sector in the economy involves shifts not only in the magnitude and direction of public and private expenditures but also in the manner in which these monies are spent. The interplay between shifting levels and patterns of expenditures and the activities carried on by government and nonprofit institutions can be briefly reviewed by considering recent trends in the expenditures for education, hospitals, and a comparatively new type of communal activity subsumed under the heading of research and development.

Table 5.7 shows us that total expenditures for education, both public and private, increased from $3.2 billion in 1930 to about $25 billion in 1960. As a percent of gross national product, educational expenditures increased from 3.5 percent in

1930 to 4.9 percent in 1960. Part of this increase reflects a more than average increase in the prices of the goods and services purchased by the education industry; it also reflects improved quality of the services provided as a result of better teachers, better textbooks, and better plant and equipment.

Table 5.7 PUBLIC AND PRIVATE EXPENDITURES ON FORMAL EDUCATION,* 1930–1960

Expenditures	1930	1940	1950	1960
	(in millions)			
Total	$3,233	$3,353	$9,335	$24,617
Public	2,655	2,756	7,312	19,282
Private	578	597	2,023	5,335
	(as percent of gross national product)			
Total	3.5	3.3	3.3	4.9
Public	2.9	2.7	2.6	3.8
Private	0.6	0.6	0.7	1.1

* Excludes capital outlay.
SOURCE: U.S. Office of Education.

Table 5.8 presents the levels of government which provide funds for public education. During the last quarter century there has been a pronounced trend toward the greater participation of Federal and state governments in the support of primary and secondary education with a corresponding decline in the share of local government. The depression of the 1930s and the consequent lowered yield from the property tax forced the states to step up their contributions. The increasing participation of the Federal government dates from 1950, largely in response to pressures of the cold war.

Certainly the contributions of the Federal government to public education would have increased much faster had it not been for two intractable political issues—the requirement of desegregation and opposition to public support for parochial schools. The former is no longer as big a political hurdle as it was, and the Federal government is constantly probing and slowly succeeding in finding ways to circum-

Table 5.8 SOURCE OF FUNDS FOR PUBLIC ELEMENTARY AND SECONDARY SCHOOLS, 1940–1960

Item	1940	1950	1960
	(in millions)		
Total	$2,260	$5,438	$14,747
Federal	40	156	652
State	684	2,166	5,768
Local	1,536	3,116	8,327
	(percent distribution)		
Total	100.0	100.0	100.0
Federal	1.8	2.9	4.4
State	30.3	39.8	39.1
Local	67.9	57.3	56.5

SOURCE: U.S. Office of Education.

vent the latter obstacle. In 1965, Congress finally succeeded in devising an acceptable formula. Henceforth, major political roadblocks to large-scale Federal support for education will no longer be present.

The recent past has witnessed a marked increase in the expenditures of all hospitals as well as striking alterations in the relative roles played by different types of hospitals in providing hospital services. The data for the decade 1952–1962 are set out in Table 5.9.

We find that total hospital expenditures rose from about $4.5 billion in 1952 to over $10 billion a decade later. Federal

Table 5.9 TOTAL EXPENDITURES OF HOSPITALS BY TYPE, 1952 and 1962

Item	1952 Amount (in millions)	1952 Percent distribution	1962 Amount (in millions)	1962 Percent distribution
All hospitals	$4,456	100.0	$10,139	100.0
Federal	925	20.7	1,408	13.9
Non-Federal, total	3,531	79.3	8,731	86.1
Long-term, total	954	21.5	1,890	18.6
Psychiatric	636	14.3	1,365	13.4
Tuberculosis	177	4.0	182	1.8
Other	141	3.2	343	3.4
Short-term, total	2,577	57.8	6,841	67.5
Voluntary	1,879	42.2	4,999	49.3
Proprietary	151	3.4	346	3.4
State and local government	547	12.2	1,496	14.8

SOURCE: American Hospital Association.

hospitals accounted for only 8 percent of the more than $5.6 billion total increase. Long-term non-Federal hospitals also sustained a relatively minor increase. The major part of the increase was due to the increase of over $4 billion in the expenditures of short-term general hospitals, about $3 billion of which was accounted for by increased expenditures by voluntary hospitals and $1 billion by those operated by state and local governments.

Since most non-Federal long-term hospitals belong to state and local governments, the decade saw the following changes: a significant decline in the relative importance of Federal hospitals in the total pattern of hospital care; no substantial change in the role of the state and local governments, but a shift from long-term to short-term care; and a marked increase in the role of voluntary short-term hospitals. The proprietary hospital was stable throughout the decade.

Since Chapter 8 will deal at length with the health services industry as a case study in the interrelations among the private, nonprofit, and governmental sectors, it is sufficient to point out here that increased expenditures for hospital care were one of the outstanding developments in the nonprofit sector in the post-World War II economy and that most of the expansion was centered around the enlarged role of the voluntary short-term general hospital. There is then significant economic activity in terms of income, employment, and output generated by the hospital industry. Hospital expenditures account for about $10 billion in a $40 billion health industry. Today, consumers spend approximately the same amount for hospital care as they do for transportation.

Governments and nonprofit institutions have long been engaged in the provision of educational and hospital services.

But since the outbreak of World War II we have seen a major new departure in government expenditures—the expansion of research and development has been a direct consequence of the vastly enlarged defense effort. The sums of money involved are very large, and the patterning of the effort has resulted in new and intricate relations between the profit and not-for-profit sectors. In fact these new relations reflect the fact that the key to effective research and development work is the quality and the number of highly trained personnel available to participate in the effort. Since private universities have always been a major center for advanced training and for basic research in the sciences, the vastly enlarged governmental programs had to be coordinated with the academic centers. But manpower considerations aside, the flow of funds for research and development is worth reviewing.

The total national expenditures for research and development at the end of World War II were very modest; the share accounted for by the Federal government amounted to $800 million or 44 percent of the total. By the time the Korean War was nearing its end, the total effort had increased to over $5 billion, with the Federal share standing at about one-half of the total. Further steep rises have occurred in the decade since the end of the Korean War, with the total reaching over $16 billion in 1962–1963. In that year the Federal share was 64 percent.

We see that the strategic factor in the rapid growth of research and development was the vastly increased sums made available by the Federal government. It should be noted, however, that during these two decades industry likewise increased substantially the scale of its own expenditures.

DEVELOPMENT, 1953-1954 and 1961-1962 *(in millions)*

Item	Research and development		Basic research	
	1953-1954	1961-1962*	1953-1954	1961-1962*
Total funds	5,150	14,740	432	1,483
Expended by Federal government	970	2,090	47	238
Source:				
Federal government	970	2,090	47	238
Expended by industry	3,630	10,870	151	403
Source:				
Federal government	1,430	6,310	19	89
Industry	2,200	4,560	132	314
Expended by colleges and universities	452	1,400	208	690
Source:				
Federal government	280	1,050	119	437
Industry	20	55	11	25
Colleges and universities	130	230	62	180
Other nonprofit institutions	20	65	16	48
Expended by other nonprofit institutions	100	380	26	152
Source:				
Federal government	60	200	10	80
Industry	20	90	4	12
Other nonprofit institutions	20	90	12	60
Sources, total	5,150	14,740	432	1,483
Federal government	2,740	9,650	195	844
Industries	2,240	4,705	147	351
Colleges and universities	130	230	62	180
Other nonprofit institutions	40	155	28	108
Expenditures, total	5,150	14,740	432	1,483
Federal government	970	2,090	47	238
Industries	3,630	10,870	151	403
Colleges and universities	450	1,400	208	690
Other nonprofit institutions	100	380	26	152

* Preliminary.

SOURCE: National Science Foundation.

103

Another facet of the expansion of the research and development effort warrants comment: the differences between the sources of funds and the locus of expenditure. Although the Federal government was the source of a high proportion of all funds, it funneled most of them to industry for development work and likewise made sizable sums available to colleges, universities, and other nonprofit institutions for research and development work under a system of contracts and grants. Of every $10 of funds that the Federal government makes available in this area, it spends only $2 in its own establishments and makes the other $8 available to the business and nonprofit sectors to carry out the investigations and development work in which it is interested.

Industry is the most important sector: in 1961 its performance of R & D work accounted for almost 70 percent of the total (Table 5.10). In addition to large sums which it invests in its own research and development, it uses even more Federal funds. It spends approximately $6 of Federal funds for every $4 of its own money. As might be expected, the major thrust of industry's efforts lies in development work. The largest share of basic research is conducted by colleges and universities. Together with other nonprofit institutions they account for about half of the total basic research effort that is currently being conducted in the United States.

These data highlight the complex new arrangements that have come to be established among the three sectors of the economy—business, government, and nonprofit—as a by-product of the vastly increased national effort to invest in new knowledge as a basis for strengthening the nation's defenses and for speeding its economic and social well-being. This expanded program would not have been possible without greatly increased government funds. But also it would not have been possible for the Federal government to spend all these funds effectively within its own establishments. It was its ability to develop new patterns of relationships with business and nonprofit institutions which made possible the rapid expansion of our national research and development effort.

We see then that the vastly increased expenditures for defense have led to a marked growth in the activities of the nonprofit sector both in terms of research and development and in broadening and deepening the scale of graduate instruction in the sciences.

While much of the expansion of the not-for-profit sector can be explained by major responses to major crises—depression and war—there is more to the story. Although it will not be possible to identify and assess all the other determinants, some of the more important will be briefly reviewed. Such a review will require a consideration of the forces that condition the role of government in fields other than defense and a consideration of the changing pattern of consumer expenditures.

Every level of government, Federal, state, and local, has long provided a series of basic services for the community at large in the fields of health, education, welfare, highways, recreation, and general government administration. Rapid increases in the population or in the distribution of the population (urbanization) as well as changes in the attitudes of the public toward the quantity and quality of the services that governments provide have important consequences for the scale of governmental activities.

An inspection of Table 5.11 may help us to identify the extent to which such factors as population increases, urbanization, a quest for more and better communal services have operated in recent years to expand the government's role in the economy. The table indicates that since 1950 there has been an almost 150 percent increase in the expenditures of government on nondefense functions. In descending order of importance the increased expenditures were centered on education, highways, utilities and liquor stores, and hospitals.

It is noteworthy that such basic functions as health, police, fire protection, sanitation, parks, and recreation all experienced a growth of well over 100 percent within the period. The tremendous increases in education were a factor both of large increases in the number of children of school age and of a pronounced desire on the part of the American public to lengthen and improve the education which children and young people receive. Increased expenditures for highways reflect the vast increase in the number of cars and in number of miles that the average citizen drives per year together with his desire to drive on better roads. The large-scale increases in "other functions" and in the conventional operations of state and local government such as police, fire protection, and parks reflect in large measure the new problems generated by accelerated urbanization and suburbanization and the pressure of the citizenry for a higher level of government services.

Passing mention should be made of the relatively slow rate of growth in four areas: postal service, welfare, utilities and liquor stores, and general control. The slower rate of growth of expenditures for welfare may be explained in part by the substantial prosperity that characterized the 1950s. But as the recent inauguration of the antipoverty program suggests, the modest rise in public welfare expenditures may also reflect temporary neglect by the electorate of the problem.

Table 5.11 TOTAL GOVERNMENT EXPENDITURES, BY FUNCTION, 1950, 1960, and 1963

Item	1950 Amount (in millions)	1950 Percent distribution Total	1950 Percent distribution Non-defense	1960 Amount (in millions)	1960 Percent distribution Total	1960 Percent distribution Non-defense	1963 Amount (in millions)	1963 Percent distribution Total	1963 Percent distribution Non-defense
Total expenditures*	$58,578	100.0	100.0	$124,360	100.0	100.0	$152,073	100.0	100.0
National defense	18,355	31.3		47,464	38.2		54,607	35.9	
Nondefense	40,223	68.7	100.0	76,896	61.8	100.0	97,466	64.1	100.0
Postal service	2,270	3.9	5.6	3,730	3.0	4.9	4,402	2.9	4.5
Education, total	9,647	16.5	24.0	19,404	15.6	25.2	24,690	16.2	25.3
State institutions of higher education	1,107	1.9	2.8	3,202	2.6	4.2	4,697	3.1	4.8
Local schools	5,879	10.0	14.6	15,166	12.2	19.7	18,738	12.3	19.2
Other	2,661	4.6	6.6	1,036	0.8	1.3	1,255	0.8	1.3
Highways	3,872	6.6	9.6	9,565	7.7	12.4	11,227	7.4	11.5
Public welfare†	2,964	5.1	7.4	4,462	3.6	5.8	5,485	3.6	5.6
Hospitals	2,050	3.5	5.1	4,213	3.4	5.5	5,077	3.3	5.2
Health	661	1.1	1.6	1,031	0.8	1.3	1,526	1.0	1.6
Police	864	1.5	2.1	2,030	1.6	2.7	2,442	1.6	2.5
Fire protection	448	0.8	1.2	995	0.8	1.3	1,195	0.8	1.2
Sanitation	834	1.4	2.1	1,724	1.4	2.2	2,041	1.3	2.1
Parks and recreation	304	0.5	0.8	770	0.6	1.0	984	0.6	1.0
General control (and financial admin.)	1,555	2.7	3.9	2,859	2.3	3.7	3,379	2.2	3.5
Utilities and liquor stores	2,739	4.7	6.8	5,088	4.1	6.6	5,885	3.9	6.0
Other	12,015	20.4	29.8	21,025	16.9	27.4	29,133	19.2	29.9

* Excludes interest and trust-fund expenditures.
† Includes welfare payments.
SOURCE: U.S. Bureau of the Census.

These brief considerations of the recent trend of nondefense expenditures by government indicate that the expansion of the government's role in the economy, while primarily a consequence of defense and defense-related pressures, was also accelerated by certain forces in the civilian sector, less spectacular but pervasive and powerful—primarily increases in population and in its density and a steady increase in the services desired by the electorate, supported by an ability and willingness to pay taxes to government or otherwise pay for these services.

The available data on consumer expenditures have limited value, however, for exploring these relationships since expenditures of nonprofit institutions, no matter what their source—consumer payments, government contracts, earnings on endowment—are counted as "consumer expenditures." As Table 5.12 indicates, total expenditures on health and medical care increased from $3.9 billion in 1940 to $26.5 billion in 1960 primarily as a result of increased spending by consumers and nonprofit organizations. While some part of this large increase reflects a disproportionate rise in the prices of medical care services, the important point is the substantial increases reflected in the number and quality of these services. Relative to the gross national product, total medical and health expenditures increased from 3.9 percent in 1940 to 5.3 percent in 1960.

The growth of the governmental and nonprofit sectors is also related to changes in personal consumption expenditures. Table 5.13, which includes the payments of government to nonprofit institutions, points up the following: a steady relative decline since 1929 in the percentage of consumer expenditures for food, clothing, and housing with a corresponding increase in personal and nonprofit expendi-

Table 5.12 EXPENDITURES FOR HEALTH AND MEDICAL CARE, 1940–1960

Item	1940	1950	1960
Total expenditures (in millions)	$3,915	$12,365	$26,503
Private and nonprofit expenditures	3,023	9,042	20,275
Public expenditures	892	3,323	6,228
Total expenditures as percent of gross national product	3.9%	4.3%	5.3%
Public health and medical care as percent of total expenditures	22.8%	26.9%	23.5%

SOURCE: U.S. Department of Health, Education, and Welfare.

Table 5.13 PERCENT DISTRIBUTION OF PERSONAL CONSUMPTION EXPENDITURES, 1929, 1950, 1960, and 1963

Item	1929	1950	1960	1963
Total*	100.0	100.0	100.0	100.0
Food, beverages, and tobacco	27.0	30.6	26.5	25.5
Clothing and accessories	14.2	12.2	10.4	9.9
Personal care	1.4	1.3	1.6	1.7
Housing	14.5	10.9	12.8	13.0
Household operations	13.6	14.9	14.0	14.0
Medical care and death expense	4.5	5.0	6.4	6.8
Personal business†	6.4	4.1	6.2	6.6
Transportation	9.6	12.5	12.5	12.6
Recreation	5.5	5.8	5.9	6.1
Private education and research	0.8	0.9	1.4	1.5
Religious and welfare activities	1.5	1.2	1.4	1.4
Foreign travel and remittance	1.0	0.6	0.9	0.9

* Includes expenditures of nonprofit institutions from payments, gifts, and contracts with businesses and governments, as well as consumers' expenditures.
† Includes legal, financial, and other personal business expenses.
SOURCE: U.S. Department of Commerce.

tures on medical care, transportation, recreation, and education. If attention is focused on the period since 1950, one is impressed in addition to the above with the increased proportion of expenditures for housing and for personal business. Over the period as a whole the relative increases in consumer expenditures for transportation, recreation, medical services, and education reflected and in turn influenced the expansion of nonprofit and governmental activities in these areas.

The preceding analysis has demonstrated that through the volume and direction of their expenditures, both governments and the consumer have contributed to the rapid growth of the not-for-profit sector. The fact that existing government and nonprofit agencies and organizations were able to expand and that new ones were established in turn reinforced the new patterns of expenditures. Through their expanded educational programs, governments and nonprofit institutions added to the supply of highly trained manpower resources, which in turn helped to reduce the scarcity value of skills. Additional trained manpower helped to keep price advances under control, and it was easier for the consumer to buy the expanded output which these additional resources helped to produce. Increased expenditures on research, highways, public health, and other basic services operated in much the same fashion. The less tangible forms of capital are playing an increasingly important role in the economy, and governments and the nonprofit organizations which are crucial in producing such capital exercise an ever more strategic influence on the shape of the economy.

But the selfsame forces also move in the opposite direction by exercising a stimulating influence on the private sector. By building roads, the government encourages the purchase of automobiles from private companies; by building airports, it encourages air travel from private airlines; and by building hospitals, it makes it possible for more sick people to receive care from private physicians. Highways, parks, marinas, and ski lifts help make the consumer's increased leisure more enjoyable. In the process of utilizing this leisure, consumers purchase more hotel space, gasoline, sports equipment, and other products of the profit-making sector.

The aim of this chapter has been to clarify the significant role that the not-for-profit sector has come to play in the changing American economy. The data that have been reviewed leave no question about the fact that the not-for-profit sector does perforce play such a role. The considerations just advanced highlight still other facets of the shifting relations among the several sectors of the economy. They have called attention to the growing importance of skill in the growth of our economy and the crucial role that government and nonprofit organizations play in the development of highly trained manpower resources.

Perhaps most important of all, the analysis has pointed up the inadequacies of any simple or static model. The not-for-profit sector does not stand by itself, apart from the private profit-seeking sector. The two are closely intertwined, and the forces which one generates are inevitably transmitted to the other. To concentrate on the recently, rapidly expanding not-for-profit sector to the neglect of dynamic forces operating in the profit sector would be as erroneous as the more conventional error of seeing all economic activity in terms of activity generated by the profit sector. The two sectors are part of an organic whole. This will be even clearer after we review the trends in employment, which is the focus of the chapter which follows.

6

Employment Trends
in the Not-for-Profit Sector

With the exception of the twelve years between 1941 and 1953 the American economy has in recent decades not been able to provide employment for all who are able and willing to work. The term "technological unemployment" dates from the latter 1920s, when the New Era was in full swing. Despite the generally prevailing prosperity, significant groups of workers in agriculture, bituminous coal, textiles, lumbering, and still other sectors experienced an erosion of employment opportunities.

The passage of the Employment Act in 1946 underscored the importance that the American public had come to ascribe to establishing and maintaining employment at a sufficiently high level so that the number of those involuntarily without work could be kept at a minimum. Nevertheless, the economy has repeatedly fallen short in recent years of meeting

113

this new national standard. If we analyze in more detail the changing patterns of employment, perhaps we will uncover some new information about which factors may be operating to keep the economy from achieving and maintaining employment at an optimum level.

Employment follows enterprise. We have just reviewed the expansion of the not-for-profit sector in terms of output and purchases; let us now assess it in terms of employment.

Table 6.1 shows us that the not-for-profit sector was characterized by a considerable growth in employment from 1929 to 1960. In 1929, 4,465,000 individuals (calculated on a full-time equivalent basis) were directly employed by governments and nonprofit institutions; they constituted 9.7 percent of the employed labor force. By 1940, employment in this sector had risen to 7,803,000 and comprised 16 percent of total employment. Only a relatively small additional increase was registered by 1950, but by 1960 both the number and percentage had again risen significantly. In that year, 13,583,000 persons, or more than one in five of all those employed, were directly employed in the not-for-profit sector.

Employment by government accounted for most of the rise. Employment in general government, which showed the more rapid growth, rose from 2,775,000 in 1929 to 10,336,000 in 1963, or from 6 percent to 14.9 percent of total employment. Government businesses increased from 409,000 employees in 1929 to 987,000 in 1963, or from 0.9 percent to 1.4 percent of total employment. Jobs in nonprofit institutions grew somewhat more rapidly than in nonprofit businesses; the nonprofit institutions almost tripled their employment between 1929 and 1960, while the employment in nonprofit businesses more than doubled.

Table 6.1 EMPLOYMENT IN GOVERNMENT AND NONPROFIT SECTORS, 1929–1960 *

Item	1929		1940		1950		1960	
	Employment (in thousands)	As per cent of total	Employment (in thousands)	As per cent of total	Employment (in thousands)	As per cent of total	Employment (in thousands)	As per cent of total
Total*†	46,216	100.0	48,486	100.0	58,731	100.0	67,305	100.0
Government and nonprofit*†	4,465	9.7	7,803	16.0	9,550	16.3	13,583	20.2
Government	3,184	6.9	6,267	13.0	7,380	12.6	10,323	15.3
General†	2,775	6.0	5,732	11.8	6,626	11.3	9,400	13.9
Businesses	409	0.9	535	1.2	754	1.3	923	1.4
Nonprofit*	1,281	2.8	1,536	3.1	2,170	3.7	3,260	4.9
Institutions	874	1.9	1,027	2.1	1,532	2.6	2,417	3.6
Businesses	407	0.9	509	1.0	638	1.1	843	1.3

*Figures include full-time equivalents.
†Includes Armed Forces and work relief.
SOURCE: U.S. Department of Commerce.

115

The rise in employment in the not-for-profit sector must be considered against the background of the changing employment patterns of the labor force as a whole. Employment data by gross industry divisions as set out in Table 6.2 provide a first approximation of the changing trends. Employment in the extractive industries has steadily declined since 1929; both agriculture and mining show absolute decreases in employment, and their combined relative share of the labor force fell from 22.1 percent in 1929 to 8.7 percent in 1960 and to 7.7 percent in 1963.

These industries demonstrated the most dramatic change, but transportation also experienced an absolute decline in employment. In 1929, 3,034,000 workers were employed in this industry. Although there have been considerable fluctuations over the years, a fairly steady drop from the end of World War II to 1963 suggests that this industry too may be in the throes of a long-term decline in employment. Major decreases have occurred in railroad employment, which was halved between 1951 and 1963, but since 1947 the work force engaged in motor freight transportation and storage has expanded. The relative share of transportation employment in the labor force dropped from 6.6 percent in 1929 to 3.9 percent in 1960 and to 3.7 percent in 1963. The ever increasing ability of Americans to drive themselves to and from work in their own automobiles must be borne in mind in interpreting these data.

Several industries have grown so slowly that their relative share of total employment has hardly changed during the past three decades. While communications and public utilities employed 1,034,000 in 1929, 1,467,000 in 1960, and 1,461,000 in 1963, their share of all employed has remained

TABLE ?? EMPLOYMENT BY INDUSTRY, 1929–1963

Item	1929	1940	1950	1960	1963
			(in thousands)		
Total	46,216	48,486	58,731	67,305	69,411
Private industries and nonprofit enterprises:	43,032	42,219	51,351	57,982	58,084
Agriculture, forestry, and fisheries	9,205	8,044	6,546	5,133	4,725
Mining	1,017	965	951	723	654
Manufacturing	10,556	11,009	15,163	16,549	16,767
Construction	2,306	1,941	3,392	4,189	4,305
Communications and public utilities	1,034	901	1,283	1,467	1,461
Transportation	3,034	2,256	2,842	2,647	2,546
Trade	7,821	8,783	11,439	13,525	13,928
Finance, insurance, etc.	1,575	1,611	2,014	2,978	3,200
Service	6,484	6,707	7,716	9,767	10,498
Government*	3,184	6,267	7,380	10,323	11,323
			(as a percent of total employment)		
Total	100.0	100.0	100.0	100.0	100.0
Private industries and nonprofit enterprises:	93.1	87.0	87.4	84.7	83.7
Agriculture, forestry, and fisheries	19.9	16.6	11.0	7.6	6.8
Mining	2.2	2.0	1.6	1.1	0.9
Manufacturing	22.9	22.6	25.9	24.7	24.2
Construction	5.0	4.0	5.7	6.2	6.2
Communications and public utilities	2.2	1.9	2.2	2.2	2.1
Transportation	6.6	4.7	4.8	3.9	3.7
Trade	16.9	18.1	19.5	20.1	20.1
Finance, insurance, etc.	3.4	3.3	3.4	4.4	4.6
Service	14.0	13.8	13.3	14.5	15.1
Government*	6.9	13.0	12.6	15.3	16.3

* Includes Armed Forces and work relief; totals are full-time equivalents.
SOURCE: U.S. Department of Commerce.

almost constant at 2.2 percent. The expansion of employment in manufacturing, construction, finance, and the service industry has been just sufficient to advance slightly the percentage of each in the total labor force between 1929 and 1963.

The share of manufacturing actually declined slightly from 1950 to 1963. If annual data in manufacturing employment from 1947 to 1963 are examined, it appears that there has been no absolute increase since 1953. From 1947 to 1953, manufacturing employment rose fairly steadily, with a total gain of 2 million within the six-year period, and a high mark of 17,549,000 was reached in 1953. Since then, manufacturing employment has fluctuated with a low of 15,945,000 in 1958 and a high of 17,243,000 in 1956. In 1964 employment in manufacturing once again reached the 1953 level. While it may be premature to conclude that manufacturing is a stable or declining industry as far as employment is concerned, the record over the past ten years has not been reassuring.

Only trade and government experienced such rapid growth that they accounted for a significantly larger proportion of the labor force in 1963 than in 1929. The outstanding change occurred in government, where employment rose from 3,184,000 in 1929 to 10,323,000 in 1960, and to 11,323,000 in 1963, or from 6.9 percent to 15.3 to 16.3 percent of total employment. The number of persons employed in trade rose from 7,821,000 in 1929 to 13,928,000 in 1963, or from 16.9 percent to 20.1 percent of the total. The industries experiencing the most rapid growth of employment are more involved in the production of services than goods.

These changes in employment patterns have affected the ranking of industries as fields of employment. Manufacturing retained first place throughout this period, but agricul-

Table 6.3 DIRECT GOVERNMENT EMPLOYMENT, 1929–1963

Item	1929	1940	1950	1960	1963
	(in thousands)				
Total employment	46,216	48,486	58,731	67,305	69,411
Government, total	3,184	6,267	7,380	10,323	11,323
Federal, total*	827	3,369	3,658	4,793	5,117
Defense	261	549	1,694	2,516	2,723
Other, except businesses	267	2,431	1,448	1,683	1,772
Businesses	299	389	516	594	622
State and local, total	2,357	2,898	3,722	5,530	6,206
Education	1,082	1,235	1,536	2,494	2,886
Other, except businesses	1,165	1,517	1,948	2,707	2,955
Businesses	110	146	238	329	365
	(as percentage of total employment)				
Total employment	100.0	100.0	100.0	100.0	100.0
Government, total	6.9	12.9	12.6	15.3	16.3
Federal, total*	1.8	6.9	6.3	7.1	7.4
Defense	0.6	1.1	3.0	3.7	3.9
Other, except businesses	0.6	5.0	2.4	2.5	2.6
Businesses	0.6	0.8	0.9	0.9	0.9
State and local, total	5.1	6.0	6.3	8.2	8.9
Education	2.3	2.6	2.6	3.7	4.2
Other, except businesses	2.6	3.1	3.3	4.0	4.2
Businesses	0.2	0.3	0.4	0.5	0.5

*Includes Armed Forces and work relief; totals are full-time equivalents.
SOURCE: U.S. Department of Commerce.

ture dropped from second place in 1929 to fifth place in 1960. Trade moved up from third to second place, and government rose from fifth to third place, while the service industry remained in fourth place from 1929 to 1960.

Table 6.1 showed us that government is clearly the most important source of employment in the not-for-profit sector. Table 6.3 shows the significant trends of expansion in overall government employment between 1929 and 1963. During the decade of the 1930s, employment by the Federal government (including persons on work relief as well as those in the Armed Forces) was the chief source of the expansion. From 1950 to 1963, however, it was the increasing employment offered by state and local governments which accounted for the major share of the expansion in government employment. Between 1950 and 1963 the growth of employment in state and local government was greater than in the Federal government; and the rate of growth of total government was substantially faster than in the economy as a whole.

When we review government employment by function without regard to the level of government, we learn that employment for national defense purposes has been the single most important activity since 1940 (Table 6.4). The number and proportion of all governmental personnel engaged in national defense, including both civilians and members of the Armed Forces, rose rapidly during the 1940s and remained high until the end of the Korean War in 1954 and then declined. Education was in second place in each benchmark year, and since 1954 it has become increasingly important as a field of government employment. Since the beginning of World War II, highways and general control activities have accounted for a declining share of total government

Table 6.4 DIRECT GOVERNMENT EMPLOYMENT BY FUNCTION, 1940, 1954, and 1962

Item	1940		1954		1962	
	Number (in thousands)	Percent distribution	Number (in thousands)	Percent distribution	Number (in thousands)	Percent distribution
Total	5,383	100.0	10,540	100.0	12,228	100.0
National defense*	1,447	26.9	4,464	42.4	3,927	32.0
Postal service	232†	4.3	504	4.8	585	4.8
Education	1,317	24.4	2,059	19.5	3,268	26.7
Highways and transportation	407	7.6	482	4.6	554	4.6
Health and hospitals	265	4.9	662	6.3	902	7.4
Police	181	3.4	281	2.7	382	3.1
Natural resources and agriculture ...	34	0.6	279	2.6	342	2.9
General control	425	7.9	508	4.8	551	4.5
Other	1,075	20.0	1,300	12.3	1,717	14.0

* Includes Armed Forces; totals are full-time equivalents.

† Source: Solomon Fabricant, "Trends in Government Activity," National Bureau of Economic Research, Occasional Paper, No. 29.

SOURCE: U.S. Bureau of the Census.

employment, while postal service and police held their own.

Additional perspective on the changing trends in employment in the not-for-profit sector can be gained from a consideration of the occupational skills of those who are employed. Table 6.5 provides an overview of the civilians who work for government by occupational group, and presents these groups as a percentage of all civilian personnel in these fields.

Several points should be noted. Professional and technical personnel accounts for the single largest component of all government employees. When managerial personnel and officials are added to the professional and technical category —and there is considerable mobility between these two fields—the professional-managerial group accounts for almost two out of every five government workers. Equally striking is the fact that in 1960, while total civilian employees of government accounted for 12 percent of all civilian employment, government employees in professional and technical occupations accounted for over 36 percent of all such personnel in the labor force. The chances were about one in three that a person who was recently trained in a professional field ended up working directly for government. Moreover, in the past two decades, during which total civilian government employment increased by over 100 percent, the relative size of these two occupational fields both as a percentage of total government employment and as a percentage of total civilian employment in these fields has remained remarkably stable.

The next largest occupational grouping is clerical: in 1960, almost one-fourth of all government employees were in this category. But marked changes have occurred in this group

Table 6.5 CIVILIAN GOVERNMENT EMPLOYEES BY OCCUPATIONAL GROUP, 1940–1960

Item	1940			1950			1960		
	Number (in thousands)	Percent distribution	As per cent of total employment in group	Number (in thousands)	Percent distribution	As per cent of total employment in group	Number (in thousands)	Percent distribution	As per cent of total employment in group
Total	3,652	100.0	8.0	5,492	100.0	9.9	7,747	100.0	12.1
Professional and technical.	1,260	34.6	37.6	1,696	30.9	34.9	2,625	33.5	36.3
Managerial and official ..	250	6.8	6.6	323	5.9	6.6	436	5.6.	8.1
Clerical	734	20.1	9.7	1,373	24.9	20.0	1,859	23.7	20.0
Craftsmen and foremen	240	6.6	4.7	492	9.0	6.4	578	8.6	7.7
Operatives	220	6.0	2.7	367	6.7	3.3	450	5.7	3.8
Service	553	15.1	16.0	837	15.2	19.6	1,294	16.5	23.7
Laborers, except farm and mine	284	7.8	9.2	338	6.2	10.0	347	4.4	11.2
Other and not reported ..	111	3.0	1.0	66	1.2	5.2	158	2.0	1.2

SOURCE: U.S. Bureau of Census. 1940 distribution adjusted to exclude Armed Forces and conform to 1950 categories.

over the past two decades within and outside of government. In 1940, government employed less than 10 percent of all clerical personnel in the economy. By 1960 government's share was up to 20 percent. This may help explain the wide-spread belief that government is overstaffed with desk workers.

Marked variations exist among the several branches of government with regard to the use of personnel with differing occupational skills. According to a recent study reported by the Senate Subcommittee on Employment and Manpower, headed by Senator Joseph S. Clark, in 1960 there were 1,066,900 civilian government workers in the five most important Federal defense agencies; they accounted for about one-seventh of all civilian government employees—Federal, state, and local. These defense agencies had a markedly lower proportion of professional and related workers than government as a whole, approximately 17 percent compared with 33.5 percent. The proportion of skilled workers, operatives, and laborers in the five defense agencies was greatly in excess of the corresponding ratio for all civilian government workers—almost 50 percent compared with 18.7 percent.

As we have seen, between 1940 and 1960 government employment increased rapidly, not only absolutely but relatively. But in 1960 government employees still accounted for only one out of eight employed persons in the nation. However, we have seen that in certain occupational fields—the professional and technical group, the clerical and service group—government provided more than its proportionate share of employment.

Because of the predominant role that professional and

Table 6.6 OCCUPATIONAL DISTRIBUTION OF PROFESSIONAL, TECHNICAL, AND KINDRED WORKERS IN GOVERNMENT, 1950 AND 1960

Item	1950			1960		
	Employment (in thousands)	Percent distribution	As percent of total in occupation	Employment (in thousands)	Percent distribution	As percent of total in occupation
Professional, technical, and kindred, total	1,696	100.0	35.0	2,626	100.0	36.3
College presidents, professors, and instructors	68	4.0	55.0	98	3.8	55.9
Engineers, technical	97	5.7	18.8	147	5.6	17.1
Lawyers and judges	24	1.4	14.1	31	1.2	14.8
Librarians	38	2.2	67.1	58	2.2	68.9
Musicians and music teachers	28	1.7	18.2	48	1.8	24.9
Natural scientists, n.e.c.	17	1.0	45.1	39	1.5	26.3
Nurses, professional	89	5.2	22.0	140	5.3	24.1
Nurses, student professional	16	0.9	20.4	10	0.4	17.9
Recreation and group workers	7	0.4	40.0	16	0.6	42.2
Religious workers	1	0.1	1.5	1	*	1.3
Social and welfare workers, except group	49	2.9	64.3	69	2.6	72.7
Social scientists	14	0.8	41.5	21	0.8	39.2
Teachers, n.e.c., elementary and secondary, n.e.c.	926	54.6	82.4	1,366	52.1	81.7
Technicians, medical and dental	15	0.9	19.0	36	1.4	26.1
Miscellaneous	307	18.2	†	545	20.7	†

* Less than .05 percent.
† Not relevant.
SOURCE: U.S. Bureau of the Census.

125

technical workers play in the operation of government, we will consider this field further. Table 6.6 shows that teachers in public elementary and secondary schools are predominant among professional and technical government workers; schoolteachers constitute over half of the total. No other single occupational group accounts for more than 6 percent of the total professional group employed in government. Engineers, professional nurses, and college instructors, professors, and presidents make up the three next largest subgroups.

When the numbers in given occupations employed in government are considered as a proportion of the total number of such workers, it can be seen that in several professions public employment is by far the most important source of jobs. Four-fifths of elementary and secondary school teachers work for government. Librarians working in public institutions account for over two-thirds of all librarian positions. Over 70 percent of all social and welfare workers (excluding those engaged in group work) in 1960 were public employees. More than half the professional personnel employed at colleges were at state or municipal universities and colleges. Over 40 percent of recreation and group workers were on government payrolls. In 1950, 45 percent of the nation's natural scientists received their paychecks from government, although by 1960 this percentage had dropped to 26 percent. However, as we shall see shortly, government funds still defrayed the salaries of many of the scientists who were working in business or nonprofit institutions.

There are other ways by which governmental employment patterns are distinctive. For instance, opportunities for women and Negroes are relatively greater in government than in other branches of the economy. As Table 6.7 shows,

Table 6.7 PROPORTION OF GOVERNMENT EMPLOYEES IN EACH OCCUPATIONAL GROUP BY RACE AND SEX, 1950 and 1960

Item	1950				1960			
	Non-whites as per-cent of total	Females as per-cent of total	Non-white females as per-cent of total females	Non-white females as per-cent of total non-whites	Non-whites as per-cent of total	Females as per-cent of total	Non-white females as per-cent of total females	Non-white females as per-cent of total non-whites
Total	8.7	37.0	8.8	37.5	11.2	40.3	11.6	41.6
Professional and technical	6.2	58.0	8.0	74.0	8.0	54.0	9.7	65.3
Managers and officials	1.6	19.2	3.1	36.6	2.8	20.6	4.7	34.1
Clerical	6.9	50.3	5.3	39.2	10.3	57.4	8.8	48.8
Craftsmen and foremen	4.7	1.5	11.6	3.8	7.3	1.7	14.4	3.3
Operatives	13.6	9.7	21.3	15.3	17.9	11.5	22.9	14.7
Service workers, except private household	14.2	28.6	21.6	43.5	17.3	36.9	22.7	48.4
Laborers, except farm and mine	22.4	1.7	26.2	1.9	25.5	1.7	33.9	2.2

SOURCE: U.S. Bureau of the Census.

127

the number of female workers as a percent of all government employees rose from 37 percent in 1950 to 40.3 percent in 1960, a very substantial share. Although the proportion of women workers in the economy at large has been growing rapidly, it is still considerably below that in the government sector: female employment as a proportion of total employment was 24.8 percent in 1940, 27.9 percent in 1950, and 32.8 percent in 1960. During the decade of the 1950s when the proportion of women in total government employment was increasing modestly, the most rapid gains occurred among service and clerical workers. There was a modest decline in the proportion of women among professional and technical employees of governments.

The growing significance of government as a source of employment for the nonwhite population is also revealed by the data in Table 6.7. Between 1950 and 1960 the proportion of total government jobs held by Negroes increased by approximately 30 percent. In 1960 the proportion of nonwhite workers in government was slightly higher than in the economy at large. More significant perhaps is the fact that there was an increase in nonwhite government workers in every occupational category from 1950 to 1960. Particularly striking were the increased proportions of Negroes among managers and officials, clerical workers and craftsmen and foremen.

Several interesting findings about Negro women workers in government can be extracted from Table 6.7. Firstly, we find that the ratio of Negro women employed to total Negro government employment increased during the decade of the fifties, a period during which there were striking increases in the total number and percentage of Negro employees in government. It appears therefore that government offered a particularly attractive employment environment for Negro women. Secondly, Negro women in every occupational category experienced more rapid gains than the total number of women workers did. Thirdly, in 1960 Negro women accounted for two out of every three Negroes in the professional and technical occupations within government, a ratio considerably greater than for all women employees. The explanation lies in the employment of a large number of Negro women teachers in the states with continuing *de facto* segregation.

Since government employment does require a high proportion of skilled and trained workers, the educational attainment of government workers is greater than that in the labor force as a whole. But even in specific occupational fields, a government worker tends to have more years of education than his counterpart employed elsewhere. This is particularly true of women and men who hold professional and managerial positions and of service workers. Government jobs are particularly attractive to educated women. In 1950, for example, about 60 percent of all employed women college graduates worked for government.

In addition to reviewing employment trends in government, we must review employment trends in the nonprofit sector in order to obtain a comprehensive view of the not-for-profit sector. The nonprofit sector consists of nonprofit institutions, such as colleges, hospitals, and religious and charitable organizations, and nonprofit businesses, such as cooperatives, mutual savings banks, and mutual insurance

Table 6.8 DIRECT EMPLOYMENT IN NONPROFIT INSTITUTIONS AND BUSINESSES, 1929–1960

Item	1929	1940	1950	1960	1963
	(in thousands)				
Total employment*	46,216	48,486	58,731	67,305	69,411
Nonprofit sector, total	1,281	1,536	2,270	3,260	n.a.
Nonprofit institutions	874	1,027	1,632	2,417	2,701
Education	287	324	442	676	755
Hospitals	} 587	} 703	502	827	959
Other			688	914	987†
Nonprofit businesses	407	509	638	843	n.a.
	(as a percent of total employment)				
Total employment*	100.0	100.0	100.0	100.0	100.0
Nonprofit sector, total	2.8	3.1	3.9	4.9	n.a.
Nonprofit institutions	1.9	2.1	2.8	3.6	3.9
Education	0.6	0.7	0.7	1.0	1.1
Hospitals	} 1.3	} 1.4	0.9	1.2	1.4
Other			1.2	1.4	1.4
Nonprofit businesses	0.9	1.0	1.1	1.3	n.a.

* Includes Armed Forces and work relief.

† Estimated.

SOURCE: U.S. Department of Commerce and the American Hospital Association.

companies. As Table 6.8 indicates, nonprofit institutions have been a more important source of employment than nonprofit businesses since 1929, and the margin has widened in recent years. The nonprofit sector in its entirety has grown from 1,281,000 full-time equivalent employees in 1929 to 3,260,000 in 1960. After rising by 20 percent between 1929 and 1940, employment in this sector increased by about 45 percent during each of the next two decades. As a proportion of total employment, the nonprofit sector grew from 2.8 in 1929 to 4.9 percent in 1960; the important gains were made in educational institutions and hospitals.

The growth of employment in the nonprofit sector can be usefully compared with the overall trends in employment in the service, trade, and finance industries as defined by the Department of Commerce. Nonprofit businesses are usually classified as either trade or finance, while nearly all nonprofit institutions fall within the category of service industry. Nonprofit businesses have accounted for only a small proportion of all employment in trade and finance: in 1929 they accounted for about one-tenth of the total, and by 1963 their share was much the same. Nonprofit institutions, on the other hand, with 2,417,000 persons on their payrolls in 1960, accounted for about one-fourth of the total employment of 9,767,000 persons in the service industry. Their share of total service employment has more than doubled since 1929.

A more detailed view of the component parts of the service industry is provided in Table 6.9. The "service industry" is narrowly defined as excluding finance, insurance and real estate, wholesale and retail trade, transportation, communications, and public utilities. It is confined to services rendered by private and nonprofit education and health institutions and certain business and consumer services, including private household workers; it excludes all government employment.

The service industry, accounting for 6,484,000 employees in 1929, showed during the depression a shrinkage in the numbers employed, which continued through 1933. Beginning to rise in 1934, employment in the industry did not pass the 1929 mark until 1940. The conclusion of World War II initiated an expansion which gained momentum after 1945. By 1960 total employment stood at 9,767,000, and it continued to rise to 10,498,000 in 1963. In 1929 the service industry accounted for roughly 14 percent of all jobs in the economy. During the next two decades the ratio declined slightly, but by 1960 it was slightly above the 1929 level. While the share of the industry in total employment did not alter, an inspection of the components of the service industry indicates that significant employment shifts took place within the industry. Large employment gains were registered primarily in the fields in which nonprofit enterprises play a conspicuous role, such as in the medical and health industry, education, and nonprofit membership organizations. Specialized business services rendered by private firms also showed a sizable gain. A marked decline took place in the number of workers in private households—from 2,348,000 in 1929 to 1,600,000 in 1960 and to 1,532,000 in 1963.

We can learn more about the trends in nonprofit employment from a consideration of certain census data. Table 6.10 presents the occupational distribution of workers in the three types of nonprofit institutions which are listed in the census as "private educational services," "welfare and religious services," and "nonprofit membership organizations."

Item	1929	1940	1950	1960	1963
	(in thousands)				
Total employment*	46,216	48,486	58,731	67,305	69,411
Private and nonprofit services	6,484	6,707	7,716	9,767	10,498
Medical and health	750	841	1,237	1,936	2,213
Education, including employment agencies	311	343	487	729	814
Nonprofit membership organizations, n.e.c.	351	390	581	831	898
Legal	194	244	234	285	312
Engineering and other, n.e.c.	83	91	157	343	381
Business, n.e.c.	209	296	497	957	1,159
Miscellaneous repair services	264	293	451	585	598
Personal services	1,008	1,050	1,225	1,284	1,321
Hotels and lodging	518	538	609	704	734
Amusement and recreation	448	421	528	513	536
Private households	2,348	2,200	1,710	1,600	1,532
	(as a percent of total employment)				
Total employment*	100.0	100.0	100.0	100.0	100.0
Private and nonprofit services	14.0	13.8	13.1	14.5	15.1
Medical and health	1.6	1.7	2.1	2.9	3.2
Education, including employment agencies	0.7	0.7	0.8	1.1	1.2
Nonprofit membership agencies	0.7	0.8	1.0	1.2	1.3
Legal	0.4	0.5	0.4	0.4	0.4
Engineering	0.2	0.2	0.3	0.5	0.5
Business, n.e.c.	0.4	0.6	0.8	1.4	1.7
Miscellaneous repair services	0.6	0.6	0.8	0.9	0.9
Personal services	2.2	2.2	2.1	1.9	1.9
Hotels and lodging	1.1	1.1	1.0	1.0	1.0
Amusement and recreation	1.1	0.9	0.9	0.8	0.8
Private households	5.0	4.5	2.9	2.4	2.2

*Includes Armed Forces and work relief.
SOURCE: U.S. Department of Commerce.

133

These census data must be used with caution. They not only include some persons employed in commercial, trade, and business schools as well as government welfare employees, but exclude the employees of two large groups of nonprofit enterprises—hospitals and nonprofit businesses. While there are alternative sources of hospital data, there are none for nonprofit business.

As Table 6.10 indicates, the majority of those employed in these three categories in both 1950 and 1960 were professional, technical, and kindred workers. The number in these groups increased from 613,000 in 1950 to 886,000 in 1960. Most of the other employees were either service or clerical workers. Reports of the American Hospital Association indicate that at least one-third of the employees of nonprofit hospitals are nurses, technicians, dietitians, therapists, or other professional and technical personnel. The large majority of other hospital personnel are service workers. Since nonprofit businesses are largely concentrated in trade and finance, their employees are probably concentrated in clerical, sales, and managerial occupations in that order.

In 1960, these three categories (private educational services, welfare and religious services, and nonprofit membership organizations) employed 12.3 percent of all professional and technical workers, almost 3 percent of all clerical workers, and 4.5 percent of all service workers. A breakdown of the specific occupations of the professional and technical workers in three nonprofit categories is found in Table 6.11. Except for a concentration of over 30 percent among elementary and secondary school teachers, no single suboccupation engaged a large proportion of the professional and technical workers in these three nonprofit categories. The distribution

Table 6.10 OCCUPATIONAL DISTRIBUTION OF EMPLOYEES IN EDUCATIONAL, WELFARE, AND RELIGIOUS ORGANIZATIONS, 1950 and 1960

Item	1950			1960		
	Number (in thousands)	Percent distribution	As percent of total in occupation	Number (in thousands)	Percent distribution	As percent of total in occupation
Total	1,116	100.0	2.0	1,706	100.0	2.6
Professional, technical, and kindred	613	54.9	12.5	882	51.8	12.3
Managers, officials, and proprietors	62	5.5	0.7	95	5.5	1.2
Clerical and kindred	166	14.9	2.4	274	16.0	2.9
Sales	6	0.5	0.2	10	0.6	0.2
Craftsmen, foremen, and kindred	29	2.6	0.4	51	3.0	0.6
Operatives	24	2.2	0.2	29	1.7	0.2
Service workers	196	17.6	3.4	326	19.1	4.5
Laborers, including farm	17	1.5	0.3	20	1.2	0.4
Occupation not reported	3	0.3	0.4	19	1.1	0.6

SOURCE: U.S. Bureau of the Census.

Table 6.11 OCCUPATIONAL DISTRIBUTION OF PROFESSIONAL, TECHNICAL, AND KINDRED EMPLOYEES IN EDUCATIONAL, WELFARE, AND RELIGIOUS ORGANIZATIONS, 1950 and 1960

Item	1950			1960		
	Number (in thousands)	Percent distribution	As percent of total in occupation	Number (in thousands)	Percent distribution	As percent of total in occupation
Professional, technical, and kindred, total	613	100.0	12.6	882	100.0	12.2
College presidents, professors, and instructors	55	9.0	44.9	78	8.8	44.1
Engineers, technical	3	0.4	0.5	3	0.4	0.4
Lawyers and judges	1	0.2	0.7	1	0.1	0.6
Librarians	14	2.2	24.0	16	1.8	19.3
Musicians and music teachers	69	11.3	44.7	101	11.4	52.7
Natural scientists, n.e.c.	1	0.2	2.7	4	0.5	2.9
Nurses, professional	9	1.5	2.3	10	1.2	1.8
Recreation and group workers	7	1.1	40.2	15	1.7	39.7
Religious workers	38	6.2	93.1	55	6.2	96.3
Social and welfare workers, except group	25	4.2	33.3	24	2.7	24.7
Social scientists	1	0.2	4.0	3	0.3	4.9
Teachers, n.e.c., elementary and secondary, n.e.c.	185	30.1	16.5	289	32.8	17.3
Technicians, medical and dental	1	0.2	1.2	2	0.2	1.5
Miscellaneous	204	33.2	*	281	31.9	*

among the suboccupations remained much the same in 1950 and 1960.

Nonprofit employment in the three categories enumerated here provided a sizable proportion of the total employment in certain occupations. Thus, 96.3 percent of all religious workers in 1960 were in these three nonprofit fields; over half of the musicians and music teachers, 44 percent of the college administrators and teachers, and almost 40 percent of all recreation and group workers also were employed in these three industries. Some occupations, on the other hand, were very sparsely represented in nonprofit employment; less than three percent of all engineers, lawyers and judges, professional nurses, natural scientists, and medical and dental technicians found employment in these three types of nonprofit institutions.

Inadequate data prevent thorough discussion of the characteristics of nonprofit employees, but some deductions can be pieced together from information provided by the Social Security System (Old Age, Survivors and Disability Insurance—OASDI). While OASDI provides both compulsory and voluntary coverage for workers in nonprofit institutions, the only data that could be broken out relate to voluntary coverage. The OASDI estimates that in June, 1963, there were some 2,170,000 persons employed in nonprofit institutions which were eligible to seek voluntary coverage for their workers. About 1,660,000 were actually covered by OASDI.

From a 1-percent sample relating to all covered employment during the year, we learn that about two-thirds of these workers in nonprofit institutions are women, that these workers frequently move between jobs in the profit and nonprofit sectors, and that only about 14 percent earn the maximum or close to the maximum wage credits under the law, $4,800 annually. About one-third have wage credits of under $600 annually. The remainder earn between $600 and $4,200, with a higher proportion in the $600 to $2,400 category. Women earn less than men: only 9 percent are in the $4,200 to $4,800 wage credit bracket compared with about one-fourth of the men, although more men than women are also found in the below $600 range.

We have seen the changing importance of the not-for-profit sector in total employment. The not-for-profit sector (government and nonprofit) employs directly more than one-half of all professional and technical workers in the economy, well over one-third of all service workers, and more than one-fourth of all clerical workers. A consideration of the relative importance of the not-for-profit sector in the net growth of employment reinforces our conclusion. Table 6.12 presents the net growth in direct employment in the not-for-profit sector as a percent of the net growth in total employment for three periods, 1929–1940, 1940–1950, and 1950–1960.

These data show that the not-for-profit sector—in fact, the Federal government alone—accounted for all of the net gains in employment from 1929 to 1940 and more than compensated for some of the net losses in the private sector. Over four-fifths of the expansion in government employment from 1929 to 1940 reflected employment by the Federal government, chiefly through work relief.

In the 1940–1950 period, the not-for-profit sector accounted for a very much smaller part of the new employment; it could take credit for less than one of five net new jobs. Government, primarily at the state and local level, and non-profit enterprises each contributed a small proportion of the new jobs. As we know, the manpower employed in the non-defense functions of the Federal government declined during these years, while the defense effort increased.

From 1950 to 1960, the not-for-profit sector accounted for nearly one out of two net new jobs in the economy. In a period characterized by neither a depression nor a major war the large gains in employment by government, amounting to one in three of all new jobs, is striking. This expansion in the not-for-profit sector was centered primarily in defense activities, state and local educational activities, governments, and nonprofit hospitals.

The significance of government as a source of new employment can be further assessed by comparing its employment expansion with that of other industries. From 1929 to 1940, the increase in net growth of government employment outdistanced that of any expanding industry. Table 6.13 shows us that while the net increase in the total labor force from 1929 to 1940 was 2,270,000, the net number of new government jobs, which were mostly work relief, was 3,083,000. These increases in government employment helped to offset the substantial decline in jobs in farming, transportation, construction, and communications.

From 1940 to 1950, government played a less important role in employment expansion; it accounted for only one out of every ten net new jobs. Manufacturing, trade, and construction showed larger absolute gains. However, the importance of government as an employer during the decade of the 1940s is minimized by these data, which do not reflect the

Table 6.12   NET GROWTH IN EMPLOYMENT IN THE NOT-FOR-PROFIT
SECTOR AS A PERCENT OF NET GROWTH IN TOTAL
EMPLOYMENT, 1929–1960

Item	1929–1940	1940–1950	1950–1960
Not-for-profit sector, total	147.0	17.0	47.0
Government, total	135.8	10.8	34.3
Federal, total*	112.0	2.8	13.2
Defense	12.7	11.2	9.6
Other, except businesses	95.3	–9.6	2.7
Businesses	4.0	1.2	0.9
State and local, total	23.8	8.0	21.1
Education	6.7	2.9	11.2
Other, except businesses	15.5	4.2	8.8
Businesses	1.6	0.9	1.1
Nonprofit sector, total	11.2	6.2	12.7
Nonprofit institutions	6.7	4.9	10.3
Education	1.6	1.2	2.7
Hospitals	} 5.1	} 3.7	3.8
Other			3.8
Nonprofit businesses	4.5	1.3	2.4

* Includes Armed Forces and work relief.
SOURCE: U.S. Department of Commerce.

employment expansion sustained during World War II,
when the government's share of total employment loomed
very large.

From 1950 to 1960, government employment increased
more rapidly than employment in any industry. Of the
8,575,000 net new jobs, government accounted for 2,943,000,
or about one in every three. The net number of new jobs in

Table 6.13 NET GROWTH OF EMPLOYMENT IN GOVERNMENT AND INDUSTRIES, 1929–1960

Item	1929–1940	1940–1950	1950–1960
	(in thousands)		
Total	2,270	10,242	8,575
Private and nonprofit, total	−813	9,134	5,632
Agriculture, forestry, and fisheries	−1,160	−1,498	−1,413
Mining	−52	−14	−228
Manufacturing	453	4,154	1,386
Construction	−365	1,451	797
Communications	−133	382	184
Transportation	−778	586	−195
Trade	962	2,656	2,086
Finance	36	403	964
Service	224	1,009	2,051
Government*	3,083	1,113	2,943
	(percent distribution)		
Total	100.0	100.0	100.0
Private and nonprofit, total	−35.8	89.1	65.7
Agriculture, forestry, and fisheries	−51.0	−14.6	−16.5
Mining	−2.3	−0.1	−2.7
Manufacturing	20.0	40.6	16.2
Construction	−16.1	14.2	9.3
Communications	−5.9	3.7	2.1
Transportation	−34.3	5.7	−2.3
Trade	42.4	25.9	24.4
Finance	1.6	3.9	11.2
Service	9.8	9.8	24.0
Government*	135.8	10.9	34.3

* Includes Armed Forces and work relief.
SOURCE: U.S. Department of Commerce.

the whole economy was smaller in the decade from 1950 to 1960 than from 1940 to 1950, but the net increase in the number of government jobs from 1950 to 1960 was two and a half times as large as from 1940 to 1950.

If it were possible to secure data on gross employment changes by industry, that is, the total number of jobs eliminated and the total number created, the results would present a more favorable picture of private enterprise, since government probably eliminated fewer positions by substituting machinery for labor. Technological improvements make possible the expansion of output without a comparable expansion in jobs. The gains from technology are easier to introduce and exploit in the production of goods than services. Since private enterprise plays the dominant role in the production of goods, the profit-seeking sector is likely to be more directly affected by advances in technology that operate to restrict the growth of jobs. Unless demand in the private sector grows very rapidly, as in fact it did in such industries as fabricated metals, electrical machinery, and chemicals, net gains in employment will be hard to achieve in the face of steady technological advances. If the rate of these advances continues, the private sector may find it very difficult to create sufficient new jobs to compensate for those eliminated.

So far this chapter has considered one aspect of the growth of the not-for-profit sector—direct employment in governmental and nonprofit organizations. There is another important facet of the growth of the not-for-profit sector: employment in the private profit-seeking sector based on the production of goods and services for the not-for-profit sector. This is usually referred to as "indirect employment."

In the discussion which follows, it should be noted that

there is often wide latitude for government either to undertake production on its own account or to purchase its requirements from others. It should also be noted that a calculation of the amount of indirect employment resulting from government purchases does not indicate whether or not these manpower and other resources might have been employed by the private sector had they been available.

Estimates of the magnitude of indirect employment resulting from the purchases from the private sector by government and the nonprofit sector are presented in Table 6.14. These estimates assume that the proportion of all employment in profit-seeking businesses devoted to the production of goods or services for nonprofit and governmental enterprises is the same as the proportion that the value of the goods and services sold to governments and nonprofit institutions by business is to the value of the total output of business. We further assume no difference in the labor input in the goods and services purchased by the not-for-profit sector from business and all other business output. Because of the gross character of these assumptions, these estimates are presented as percentages rather than as absolute numbers of workers.

The Federal government undertook to estimate the indirect employment effect of government expenditures in the *Manpower Report of the President* for 1963. It calculated that 6.5 million people held jobs in the private sector as a result of the $62 billion of government expenditures as follows: 3.3 million jobs as a result of Federal expenditures for defense, 0.5 million in other Federal programs, and 2.7 as a result of state and local expenditures. The *Manpower Report* explains that the estimates of employment "are not limited to the prime contractors but also include subcontractors and suppliers of materials.... However, these estimates do not make any allowance for the further generation of employment through respending of wages and other income (the multiplier effect), nor for the labor required to make the capital equipment consumed in production."

Prepared by the Senate Subcommittee on Employment and Manpower in 1962, an estimate of employment in private industry stemming from the production of defense-related goods and services totaled 2,905,000, with a relative overrepresentation in the occupational distribution of craftsmen and operatives. Indirect employment in the private sector resulting from goods and services purchased by governments is, as Table 6.14 shows, considerably more important than employment growing out of purchases made by nonprofit institutions. In 1960 the employment in the private sector generated by the not-for-profit sector amounted to 11.4 percent of total employment, more than double the proportion in 1929.

If one adds the direct employment offered by the not-for-profit sector and the indirect employment attributable to the expenditures of not-for-profit enterprises in the private sector, the combined direct and indirect employment in and for the not-for-profit sector accounted for 15.1 percent of total employment in 1929 and rose to 31.5 percent by 1960. Governments' share increased from 10.6 percent in 1929 to 24.8 percent in 1960; nonprofit institutions and businesses made up the remainder (Table 6.15).

To illuminate the impact of the not-for-profit sector on the expansion of employment, Table 6.16 presents the net change in direct employment in and indirect employment for the not-for-profit sector from one decade to the next as a

Table 6.14 INDIRECT EMPLOYMENT FOR THE NOT-FOR-PROFIT
SECTOR IN THE PRIVATE SECTOR AS A PERCENT OF
TOTAL EMPLOYMENT, 1929–1960

Item	1929	1940	1950	1960
Total	5.4	6.9	7.4	11.4
Governments	3.7	5.6	5.8	9.4
Nonprofit institutions	1.7	1.3	1.6	2.0

SOURCE: Based on data from U.S. Department of Commerce.

percentage of the net change in total employment. In the period 1929 to 1940, the net increase in direct and indirect employment for the not-for-profit sector was almost twice as
large as the net growth in total employment.

The not-for-profit sector played a much more modest role
in the 1940–1950 decade when it accounted for only 26 percent of the net increase in total employment. From 1950 to
1960, the share of the not-for-profit sector in employment expansion was again substantial; it accounted for over 85 percent of the total. We also see that not only is government the
largest component of the not-for-profit sector but it has accounted for most of the expansion in this sector in both direct and indirect employment.

There is no blinking the fact that in two out of the last
three decades the not-for-profit sector accounted for the largest part of the total expansion of employment. Between 1950
and 1960 the sector accounted directly and indirectly for almost nine out of every ten new jobs added to the economy.
The fact that this sector loomed so important on the employment front in recent decades cannot be ignored or minimized. But neither should it be exaggerated. It does not follow that if the not-for-profit sector had grown more slowly

Table 6.15 DIRECT AND INDIRECT EMPLOYMENT IN AND FOR THE
NOT-FOR-PROFIT SECTOR AS A PERCENT OF TOTAL
EMPLOYMENT, 1929–1960

Item	1929	1940	1950	1960
Total	15.1	23.0	23.7	31.6
Governments*	10.6	18.5	18.4	24.8
Nonprofit institutions	3.6	3.4	4.2	5.5
Nonprofit businesses	0.9	1.1	1.1	1.3

* Includes Armed Forces and work relief.
SOURCE: Based on data from U.S. Department of Commerce.

Table 6.16 NET CHANGE IN EMPLOYMENT IN AND FOR THE NOT-
FOR-PROFIT SECTOR AS PERCENT OF NET CHANGE IN TOTAL
EMPLOYMENT, 1929–1960

Item	1929–1940	1940–1950	1950–1960
Not-for-profit sector, total	183.9	26.8	85.5
Direct employment	147.0	17.0	47.0
Indirect employment	36.9	9.8	38.5
Governments	179.6	17.5	68.6
Direct employment*	135.8	10.8	34.3
Indirect employment	43.8	6.7	34.3
Nonprofit institutions	−0.2	8.0	14.5
Direct employment	6.7	4.9	10.3
Indirect employment	−6.9	3.1	4.2
Nonprofit businesses—direct	4.5	1.3	2.4

* Includes Armed Forces and work relief.
SOURCE: Based on data from U.S. Department of Commerce.

or not at all, the manpower resources utilized in this sector
might not have been absorbed in the private sector. That
they would have been absorbed in part is almost certain; that
they would have been completely absorbed remains moot.

7

Defense Contracting: Aerospace

The burden of the foregoing analysis has been to highlight the innovations in enterprise structures that have characterized our dynamic economy during the past several decades. Striking among the innovations has been the emergence of a new pattern of relations between the private and the governmental sectors in the field of defense contracting. While we continue to classify most defense contractors in the private sector because they are profit-seeking undertakings, their methods of operation vary markedly from those of most private corporations. Instead of unilaterally determining what to produce, they must await the decision of government officials. Instead of selling their output in a competitive market, they sell almost all of it to the Federal government. Instead of retaining as profits their revenues in excess of costs, they may have to return all above a negotiated sum to the government. In short, it is the government rather than the competi-

147

tive market which determines their profitability, even their survival.

This chapter will seek to delineate some of the major characteristics of one large group of defense contractors—the aerospace companies—and to assess some of the important policy considerations that flow from this new pattern of conducting business. Particular attention will be focused on the implications for manpower utilization. In the absence of an agreement about the boundaries of the aerospace industry, we have relied primarily on the data compiled and published by the industry's own trade association.

The Armed Forces have long depended on the private enterprise sector of the economy for most of the goods which they use, both in peace and in war. Although the Navy operates a limited number of shipyards and the Army a limited number of arsenals, the primary mission of these service establishments is that of research and development and quality and cost control. This tradition helps to explain why the Navy manufactured aircraft in World War I and why the Army has sought to advance its explorations into space at the Redstone Arsenal. Nevertheless, the Armed Forces have always looked to private enterprise for most of their procurement, including their procurement of weaponry. Hence the question arises, what is new or special about their relations to the aerospace companies?

The answer is both quantitative and structural. In the years preceding the outbreak of World War II, the total expenditures of the Army and the Navy were at a rate of approximately $1 billion annually, out of a total of about $9 billion of Federal expenditures when the gross national product averaged about $90 billion. The comparable data for 1963 are: $53 billion for expenditures for national defense (with an additional $7 billion for atomic energy and space) out of a total of $93 billion of Federal expenditures, with a gross national product of $585 billion. These figures imply that prior to World War II the economic impact of defense spending was comparatively insignificant; it comprised a little more than 1 percent of the gross national product. Today it is almost 10 percent.

While we could find in our history some parallels to each of these circumstances and conditions, together they represent a unique constellation. A few additional figures will help to set the stage. About half of the expenditures of the Department of Defense, which total more than $50 billion annually, is for personnel and operations and maintenance. Most of the remainder is devoted to procurement, including contracts for research and development. Of the $26 billion prime contract awards in 1962, about $19 billion went for "hard goods": aircraft, missiles systems, electronic and communications systems, ships, tanks, weapons. Roughly 80 percent of the $19 billion was spent for aircraft, missiles, and electronics.

The last years have witnessed a marked shift in the relative expenditures of the Department of Defense between end items and research, development, test, and evaluation (RDT&E). In 1956, these RDT&E awards accounted for less than 14 percent of all prime contracts; in the last five years the proportion has risen to between 22 and 25 percent.

The scale of these government purchases alone would justify the contention that the post–World War II pattern of defense contracting represents a unique departure in the structure and functioning of the American economy. The extent to which this pattern is in fact different from that characteristic of most private enterprise is reinforced by the following:

1. The Federal government increasingly purchases research and development potential rather than hardware, and in this it cannot guide its procurement by the same rules and regulations that it has developed over the years for the purchase of conventional weaponry.

2. The uncertain international situation means that the government must be concerned not only about the procurement of a single item or weapons system but about the maintenance of a total defense capability that can be sustained only through continuing large-scale purchases.

3. The scientific and financial management of the current large-scale programs that involve the rapid exploitation of new scientific ideas and technology is without precedent.

4. The fact that the government lets the contracts and pays the bills inevitably opens the decision-making processes to a large number of political considerations and pressures.

5. Inherent in the strenuous efforts that are being made to advance the science and art of weaponry is the fact that relatively little stability can be introduced into contracting relationships between the government and the aerospace companies. Defense contracting is characterized by increasing instability.

There are several different ways of looking at the significance of defense procurement for the economy. In terms of total sales of manufacturing companies, defense production accounted for only somewhat over 6 percent in 1962. As a proportion of durable goods alone, defense production accounted for over 8 percent. But the impact on particular industries, areas, and companies is very much greater. For instance, all ordnance production and 94 percent of aircraft production is for defense. The proportion of total ship production which is earmarked for defense is about 60 percent. And even in such a basic civilian industry as electrical machinery, about 20 percent of total output is for military purposes.

With respect to regions and states, defense production is very heavily concentrated in the Southwest and the West. Although most of the large industrial states of the East and Middle West are engaged in defense production, including research and development, the significance of this effort is much less than in the several Western states where it accounts for one-quarter of all manufacturing employment.

Another measure of the significance of defense contracts on particular industries and companies is the fact that between one-fifth and one-third of the sales of leading manufacturing companies outside of the aircraft industry, such as General Electric, Westinghouse, Philco, Farm Machinery and Chemical, and Minneapolis-Honeywell, represents sales to the Federal government.

One additional facet of the defense business should be briefly noted at this point. In 1962 just under three-quarters of all prime contracts were let to 100 large corporations. Small businesses, which are defined as those having less than 500 employees, received somewhat less than one-fifth of all prime contracts awarded. Even when allowance is made for the fact that small business receives a substantial number of subcontracts, the extent to which defense work is concentrated in large organizations is pronounced.

These then are the parameters of defense procurement,

particularly those defining aerospace. And these are some of the implications that flow therefrom.

1. The survival and profitability of the areospace companies are dependent on new contracts from the government.

2. The heavy concentration of the aerospace industry in a few areas makes the economy of these areas very heavily dependent on new contracts.

3. The sudden cancellation of large defense contracts can have a disastrous effect on particular companies and communities.

4. Since the awarding of contracts and, when necessary, the cancellation of defense contracts must be made by government officials and since these decisions frequently have a life or death influence on the economic future of particular groups, it is inevitable that the officialdom is subjected to a great deal of pressure.

At the outbreak of World War II total employment in the aircraft industry amounted to slightly more than 60,000. By the time the United States entered the war, it had risen to half a million, or roughly an eightfold increase in two years. By the end of 1943 the total was approaching 1.5 million, or a further threefold increase in two years and a twenty-five-fold expansion in four years. By V-J Day the total had shrunk to 325,000, and by 1948 a further decline had reduced it to about 235,000; a decline of about 85 percent took place in five years. By the time of the outbreak of hostilities in Korea the total had climbed to 280,000; thereafter it grew rapidly and reached about 800,000 as the conflict neared its end. By 1957 the figure had crept upward to just short of 900,000. Since then, a slow but steady decline has been taking place. By the end of 1961 total employment in the aircraft industry was about 670,000.

These gross figures include some important qualitative changes. At the height of the World War II expansion, nine out of every ten aircraft employees were production workers. By the time of Korea, only seven of every ten workers were in production; the ratio of engineering and technical personnel had increased substantially. By 1959 less than half of the work force were production workers. The latest figures indicate a further decline; today the proportion is in the neighborhood of 40 percent.

The shift from long-run production of relatively simple aircraft to very short-run production of highly complex jets and the increasing stress on unique spacecraft and on research and development have been reflected in a marked increase in the proportion of both technical and white-collar personnel. Currently, technical personnel, including scientists and graduate engineers as well as draftsmen and engineering aides, account for 25 percent of the work force. The white-collar group below the managerial level accounts for almost the same proportion. The rest are classified as in the management group. To recapitulate in percentage terms: management, 12 percent; technical personnel, 25 percent; white collar, 23 percent; production workers, 40 percent.

The rapid growth in the numbers of professional personnel employed in aerospace companies is indicated by the following selective data. In 1954 the total number of scientists and engineers was approximately 28,000; by 1960 the total was about 65,000—an increase of slightly more than 130 percent. The percentage increase in certain categories of scientists was considerably larger: the most conspicuous rise was the fivefold increase in physicists and the fourfold increase in mathematicians. These two groups combined increased from under 2,000 to over 8,000 in four years. It is worth noting that roughly two-thirds of all scientists and engineers in aerospace are employed in research and development.

We have already alluded to the extent to which employment in aerospace and, more broadly, in defense is heavily concentrated in a relatively few states and regions. With respect to manpower, we see that in 1960 the three states that comprise the Pacific region had an aerospace payroll of just under $1.9 billion, out of the national total industry payroll of about $4.6 billion, or roughly 40 percent. During the preceding five years, a marked shift occurred in the rate of growth and decline of the several regions: the proportion of total defense output produced by the industrial heartland of America—Ohio, Indiana, Illinois, Michigan, and Wisconsin —was reduced by about 20 percent, while the proportion produced by the Western states, particularly Colorado, increased threefold. The West Coast pushed its relative share higher, as did New England, by about 10 percent.

Another indication of heavy concentration of defense industry is the fact that in two states, Washington and Kansas, employment in defense institutions accounts for over 25 percent of all manufacturing employment, and in five Western states—California, Arizona, New Mexico, Utah, and Colorado—it accounts for between 15 and 25 percent. The national average is approximately 7 percent.

The substantial fluctuations in total employment and the changes in recent years in the occupational mix suggest that the turnover rate must be relatively high. And so in fact it has been. Accessions have been running between 25 and 30 per 100 per year, and separations have fluctuated between 30 and 40 per 100 per year.

The manpower position that emerges from this review is one of large-scale total employment fluctuating widely over the years, heavily concentrated in the West and Southwest, shifting rapidly from a predominance of production workers to technical and white-collar workers, with recent rapid increases in the number and proportion of scientists and engineers assigned primarily to research and development work.

A large number of beliefs and convictions critical of the aerospace industry have currency. But each of the presumed shortcomings must be assessed in terms of the unique characteristics of the aerospace industry. One charge is that many projects which are initiated fail before they reach fruition— there is an estimate of $6 billion in canceled missile projects. But there is no way of developing significant breakthroughs in weaponry without taking major risks. While many missile projects have failed, the Polaris program and many others have proved successful. Uncertainty is a basic characteristic of the industry.

A second charge supported by a considerable amount of testimony, including the considered opinion of former President Eisenhower, emphasizes excess capacity. Each service strives constantly for a larger share of the defense dollar, and the defense contractors are their powerful allies. Congressmen from the districts and states that are likely to profit from the appropriations often represent a particularly strong phalanx in advancing the claims of the partisans.

There is no justification for maintaining excess capacity. Nevertheless, Congress does face difficulties in arriving at a

156 *The Pluralistic Economy*

determination of the capacity necessary to cope with present and prospective requirements. Although it would be unwise for the government to become dependent on one or even two contractors, it does not follow that all firms that were at one time involved in defense production ought to be kept indefinitely afloat. Yet the letting of contracts to firms in the aerospace industry over these past years conveys the impression that powerful forces are operating to maintain an unnecessarily expanded production capability. Such excess capacity tends to waste dollars and manpower. The rapidly rising defense appropriations of recent years made it relatively easy to protect the excess capacity. If the defense budget levels off or declines, the pressure at least from the Department of Defense for corrective action will increase, because the Department will pay closer attention to its reduced budget.

The present expanded production capability has led the principal competitors to devote a significant proportion of their time and energy to the task of bidding on a great many contracts in the hope of being awarded the one in seven or so which the company must have if it is to survive. As the TFX controversy made clear, the bids are so nearly equivalent that it is exceedingly difficult for the government to reach a determination of potential differentials in performance and price. In such circumstances there is wide scope for political forces to affect the final determination.

To some extent considerations other than market price and performance have been written into law and administrative regulation; these include the set-asides for small business, special advantages for depressed areas, and the obligation of all large government contractors to pursue nondiscriminatory policies with respect to the hiring, training, promotion, and separation of their personnel. These provisions imply that the Federal government, engaged in more than the single mission of securing the best defense for the least dollars, is willing within certain narrowly defined limits to use its procurement dollars to assist in the realization of other objectives, such as decreasing the rate of unemployment in particular localities or increasing the employment opportunities of minority groups. It is exceedingly difficult, if not impossible, to draw up an accounting system that would reveal in dollar and manpower terms whether these additional objectives have resulted in a net social gain or loss. But this much is certain: As the number and variability of the criteria increase, it is more difficult for the awarding agency to reach an objective determination.

A summary judgment of these efforts at this time is that the Department of Defense has found it very difficult to increase materially the share of the procurement dollar which goes to depressed areas or small business, but it has made considerable progress in the last few years in eliciting the co-operation of the larger contractors in expanding employment opportunities for minority group members.

Beyond these specific social objectives there is another aspect of defense procurement that carries broad implications for manpower utilization. We have noted that the awarding of contracts to particular firms or their cancellation frequently results in substantial changes in the economic life and particularly the employment patterns of the communities in which the prime contractor and principal subcontractors are located. In many instances when a contract is let, the community must build or expand its public and private facilities to cope with the added population and labor force.

Expansion is generally a pleasant, even an exhilarating experience. The secondary costs are relatively easy to absorb. But contraction is the reverse.

When the Skybolt program was terminated in 1963, over 5,200 people were laid off within a month and a half. About 3,000 were let go by Northrop Nortronics at Hawthorne, California, and Douglas Aircraft released the remainder, most of whom were professional, clerical, or skilled workers. With employment relatively strong on the Coast, this cutback was absorbed without too much difficulty. But the question arises about the consequences that would follow upon a cutback which would affect several major programs at the same time. Such a development could undermine the economic foundation of an area in short order.

The serious local disturbances that can follow upon a cutback help to explain why government officials are loath to cancel a program until they are forced to. Moreover, every cutback and cancellation carries with it implicit criticism of its original protagonists and sponsors as well as those who had the responsibility for monitoring it along the way. It is easier for a large bureaucratic structure, especially one which may face eventual congressional inquiry, to let matters slide in the hope that time will somehow take care of the problems rather than to take action which carries with it overt acknowledgment of error or failure.

These are some of the complex factors in the nature of an aerospace industry operating within a governmental contracting structure that make it difficult indeed to avoid situations where scarce manpower resources tend to be ineffectively utilized. But this is but one dimension of a two-faceted problem. We must also consider the impact of government contracting on manpower utilization from the vantage point of the individual aerospace company.

As noted earlier, the rapid advances in military and space technology and the increasing costliness of weapons systems have made it even more important that government reach sound decisions about which technological leads to follow up and which to eschew. But, unlike the purchase of commodities in established markets, the government is not able to assess the relative advantages of these systems since they generally do not exist, but must be designed and developed. The task of the government here actually is to assess the relative research and development potential of competing concerns.

This task has important manpower implications. Since it is short of competent research and development personnel in its own ranks, the government has sought to broaden and deepen its ability to make sound judgments through a series of devices that include heavy reliance on contracting with nonprofit institutions to help in the blueprinting of new approaches and in the assessment of competing proposals. The government has also made heavy use of expert consultants from academic life and the business community. While these efforts of the government have been as necessary as they have been sound, this approach does have limitations. The number of qualified consultants in a specialized field is relatively small, and almost all have some stake direct or indirect in the matters concerning which they give advice. There is considerable competition among profit-seeking aerospace companies, the universities, and various specialized nonprofit defense organizations for the research and development dollar.

Thus the government is left with some only partially resolved problems. It still faces serious difficulties in selecting competent advisers. It still must convince these busy outsiders to devote the time and energy to the task of consultation. Then it faces the possibility either that the advisers will rubber-stamp the proposals and recommendations passed by the staff or that they will become burdensomely operative. The fact that no consultant group ever has the final responsibility introduces still another factor which impedes an effort to raise the quality of performance, since performance depends on a close relation between authority and responsibility. Finally, most governmental agencies find it difficult to attract and hold senior scientific-administrative personnel to carry the primary responsibility for overseeing the major programs.

Conflicts of interest aside, and they can never be completely put aside in a relatively small scientific-management community where each decision is important for the reputation of the individuals concerned and for the prestige or profits of the institutions concerned, there are serious shortcomings as well as important advantages in the consulting system which is an integral part of the larger system of defense contracting.

In addition to selecting the contractors who are more likely to be able to overcome the multiple obstacles in the design and development of new weapons systems or in significant modifications of old ones, the Department of Defense must also attempt to shorten the time period between obligation and execution. And nothing has a more unsettling effect on the utilization of manpower than a crash program. In recent testimony on the military supply system, Secretary McNamara delineated several very costly errors, each of which reflected the government's determination to push ahead in production before basic problems of development had been solved. The desire for speed without adequate consideration of other criteria meant that large sums of money as well as many man-years of scientific and skilled manpower were wasted.

But time is a crucial aspect of the mission of the Armed Forces; often what might at first appear to be wasteful use of manpower may in fact be justified in terms of the strategic objective. The contractor who had the responsibility of making the Atlas bases operational originally programmed the work so that a limited number of teams would be in the field. Each would move to a new base as it finished its work at an existing base, thereby conserving manpower, equipment, transportation, and other costly resources. But the authorities in Washington decided that speed was of the essence, and the manpower and other costs were thereby increased by a very large factor.

Implicit in work at the frontiers of applied science and technology is the almost certain shortage of individuals with the needed range of competences and skills. A broad band of competence and skill in a work force usually reflects experience, and by definition there is little or no experience in projects at the frontiers. One particular group which is scarce is the project directors—men who have the combination of skills, technical and administrative, to oversee large teams of specialists. Since there is only a relatively small number of qualified project managers, it follows that much of the work of defense firms will be inadequately supervised and many hours of human effort and many millions of dollars will be ineffectively used. The essence of this difficulty lies in the nature of the work that the aerospace companies are engaged in, but the nature of the contractual relationships with the government and the related personnel systems plays a part here. The government has not yet been able to establish the type of long-range financing, even of research and development, that would enable the major contracting companies to offer the long-run career opportunities and security which are important to the scientific and engineering communities. Moreover, the instability of the contractual relationships, compounded by the excess capacity of the industry, has led to less than an optimal distribution of scarce manpower resources. And when the available talent is poorly distributed, those whose work depends on the creative few will also be less than fully effective.

Major deviations from the competitive market are inherent in the nature of the aerospace industry. The questions that remain open are whether past policies and positions can be modified to provide for a more effective use of resources, including manpower resources, within the framework of other major national, political, and social objectives. Some of the key issues will be raised below, not in expectation of providing answers, but in order to point directions for further research and evaluation.

These are the constituent elements out of which an improved pattern of manpower utilization must be fashioned. Aerospace is an industry with large capital costs. It is an industry that has come increasingly to depend on a special occupational mix: the proportion of scientific and technical personnel in its total work force is very high. This group is concerned not only about their present terms of employment but also about their career prospects and the outlook for career stability. The projects which the industry is engaged in are characterized by very high risks. Increasingly, specific programs have a relatively short life, which contributes still further to the risk; no longer can a company look forward to long production runs to help cover high development costs. Most of the key decisions must be made within an administrative environment in which political forces have great play and in which the administrator is handicapped by the absence of the usual criteria of a competitive market. These are the realities of defense contracting in aerospace; improvements can be made only as these realities can be brought under more effective control.

Most economists would agree that substantial excess capacity supported by public or private funds will inevitably result in the widespread wasteful use of resources. Most political scientists would agree that it is difficult to secure speedy legislative and administrative support for cutting back government installations once they become redundant. The first question that arises, then, is the extent to which mechanisms exist to make a sensible determination of the amount of capacity required to meet the present and prospective needs of the government for defense; the second is how to develop mechanisms which will shrink that capacity if it is found to be excessive. Unless there is a reasonable balance between capacity, including standby capacity for emergency need, and requirements, the waste of manpower and other resources will be substantial.

Closely related to the foregoing is the question of the adequacy of existing mechanisms to help guide the allocation of prime contracts among different firms and different localities. It is reasonably clear that the gravamen of decision-making has been in terms of current research and production capability because of the Defense Department's inevitable concern with time. This has led to heavy concentration both corporate and geographic. Yet as the period of the cold war lengthens, there may be opportunity to draw up a comprehensive balance sheet in which social costs and benefits previously excluded from the decision-making process are included. The Federal government has heavy responsibility beyond defense, and its defense and space procurement policies affect the reduction of unemployment, the opportunity of minority groups to secure employment, the restraining of excessive corporate power, the broadening of the nation's research potential, and still other important national goals. The objective should be to improve the balancing of short- and long-run considerations in which the primary concern of defense and space procurement is considered within a more complete framework, which will include such factors as whether the defense capability of the United States could be made stronger as a result of alterations in the present pattern of procurement.

The burden of this analysis has been to emphasize that since the end products of aerospace are used overwhelmingly by government, since the prices are negotiated by government, since the profits are determined by government, the government has, or surely could have, the major role in determining how the industry uses its manpower resources. Considerable evidence suggests that there is marked scope for improvement on many fronts and that the government must soon assume greater responsibility for assessing the broader aspects of manpower utilization in aerospace because of its importance both for defense and for economic growth and stability.

The burden of this chapter has been to reveal the very considerable flexibility that the American economy has demonstrated in developing new relations between government and the profit sector in meeting the unparalleled demands for the establishment and maintenance of a strong defense industry. This review has also called attention to the need for improving the several political-administrative mechanisms that must perforce assume much of the responsibility, ordinarily carried by the competitive market, for determining the allocation of scarce resources and determining what these resources are entitled to earn.

8

Expansion of Nonprofit Enterprise: The Health Services Industry

The medical and health services industry is an outstanding example of the commingling of private, nonprofit, and governmental action. The physician, more than any other individual, determines the way in which health services are produced and distributed. Most physicians are self-employed and operate within the private sector. On the other hand, nonprofit hospitals, rather than institutions under the control of government or private entrepreneurs, for many decades have met most of the community's need for hospital services, particularly short-term care. Governments have long played an important role in the provision of health care, particularly with respect to the prevention and control of infectious and contagious diseases and to providing minimum care for the poor.

No individual, no matter how wealthy he is, can assure his

own good health. His freedom from disease will depend in considerable measure on whether the causes of disease have been controlled within the community, the region, and the nation in which he lives. A citizenry interested in good health must have recourse to government for many essential services.

The large-scale involvement of government and nonprofit institutions in the provision and distribution of health and medical services also reflects the values imbedded in our tradition. We believe that the sick and injured are entitled to help, irrespective of whether they can afford to pay for it.

These several factors help to explain the participation of each of the three sectors—private, nonprofit, and government—in the health industry. From colonial days each has played a significant role.

This chapter will describe the pattern that currently exists and the direction in which it may evolve. Let us begin by setting forth some basic measures of the scale of the health industry.

In 1960 about 2.6 million persons were directly employed in the health services industry. It thus became the third largest grouping—after agriculture and construction and a little ahead of public education. Total expenditures for health and medical care increased from 3.6 to 5.7 percent of the gross national product between 1929 and 1961. Even during the depressed 1930s, employment in the medical and health services expanded by nearly 15 percent. Subsequently, employment grew even more rapidly; it increased by nearly 60 percent during the 1940s, and by 54 percent during the 1950s.

These figures reflect only the increases in the numbers of personnel employed in organizations providing medical, health, and related services. No account has been taken of the large numbers who contribute to the increased standard of medical care, such as members of the Armed Forces who provide medical and related services to military personnel or those who work in industrial or educational organizations not primarily devoted to the provision of medical or health services. One recent estimate of the United States Public Health Service places this number at approximately half a million.

Also excluded are an estimated half million or more persons directly or indirectly employed in industries related to the provision of health and medical services, such as employees engaged in the manufacture and sale of pharmaceuticals. The civilian labor force directly and indirectly involved in the provision of health and medical services actually amounts almost to 4 million, but even the lower figure of 2.6 million directly engaged in the medical and health industry establishes the fact that this industry currently occupies a major place in the American economy. Moreover, it is a rapidly expanding industry. During the fifties, only public education among the industries with at least 1 million employees in 1950 had a faster rate of growth.

The rapid growth of the health industry since the 1930s reflects the interaction of a number of forces. Scientific and technological advances, such as newly devised surgical methods and anesthesiology, held forth the promise of significant gains to the public. But before they could be realized, the number and quality of general hospitals had to be substantially expanded and the citizenry had to be able to pay for the costs of increased hospitalization. The innovation of nonprofit and commercial systems of hospital insurance plans and shortly thereafter of medical insurance plans, particularly Blue Cross and Blue Shield, provided a new enterprise structure which enabled consumers to prepay their costs of hospitalization. This new mechanism made possible the substantially enlarged flow of consumer payments for hospital care and, in turn, assisted nonprofit hospitals in coping more effectively with the enlarged demand for their services by underpinning their operating resources and reducing their dependence on philanthropy.

Government, in light of its traditional responsibility to provide services to special categories of patients, increased the scale of its support for state mental hospitals, veterans' hospitals, and hospitals providing care for members of the Armed Forces and their dependents. In addition, it broadened its clinic services and provided funds for the health and medical care of additional groups of persons such as crippled children. The Federal government also undertook several new roles. It entered upon the large-scale subsidization of the construction of new hospitals and health clinics in association with state and local governments and voluntary organizations. It became the major sponsor of medical research and contributed markedly to the training of specialized personnel.

The greatly intensified efforts of the Federal government with respect to supporting hospital construction, research, and the training of personnel, instead of reducing, stimulated the efforts of state and local governments as well as of nonprofit and business organizations to increase their support.

Another illustration of the dynamic interaction among the several sectors of the health industry—this time with the nonprofit sector in the lead—can be found in the developments subsequent to the introduction of Blue Cross. Developed to meet the needs of consumers as well as hospitals, the Blue Cross idea grew rapidly during the Depression, especially after it was endorsed by the American Hospital Association, which has played a major role in its growth and initial operation. Beginning as a community plan, Blue Cross was able to tap the vast market for hospital insurance presented by employee groups. The quick success of Blue Cross paved the way for the Blue Shield programs which cover, at least in part, the costs of physicians' services in connection with a hospitalized illness.

The demonstration by Blue Cross and Blue Shield that insurance for hospital, surgical, and medical expenses was feasible encouraged private and mutual insurance companies to expand their activities dramatically during and after World War II. They have been especially successful in tailoring plans to the needs of different employer and employer-union programs and in developing plans to cover major medical expenses. The amount of insurance underwritten by commercial and mutual insurance companies now exceeds the volume of the nonprofit plans. The fact that the private companies were able to adjust their rates according to the experience of their subscribers in the use of hospitals meant that they soon had a pronounced competitive advantage over the community-oriented Blue Cross plans, which for the most part sought to provide the same range of benefits for all subscribers irrespective of their medical experiences.

Hospital insurance, the most usual form of health insurance, was held by only 9 percent of the population in 1940; in 1960, 74 percent were insured. During this period, the proportion who were covered for the expense of physicians' services in hospitals increased from 2 to 49 percent. By 1960, the outlays for profit and nonprofit insurance programs accounted for 24 percent of nongovernmental expenditures for health and medical services. Impressive as this growth in prepayment plans has been, direct payments for physicians' and health services still account for over two-thirds of all private expenditures and half of all payments for medical and health services.

Although there had been earlier experiments, the Social Security Act of 1935 marked the emergence of an elaborate system of Federal grants-in-aid for a wide variety of medical services at the state and local level. Federal aid both supplemented and encouraged the expansion of other public, nonprofit, and private financing of medical services. Each of the Federal programs has had a specific focus—vocational rehabilitation, crippled children, maternal and child health, venereal disease, tuberculosis, heart conditions, cancer, etc. State and local governments, along with charitable groups and nonprofit hospitals, have always played a large role in the care of the medically indigent. Recently, Federal, state, and local governments have made payments out of public welfare funds to persons and institutions providing medical care to the indigent, and this program now accounts for over 8 percent of all public expenditures for health and medical care.

World War II helped to make the United States much more aware of the costs of mental illness and the potentialities of psychiatric care. One million young men were adjudged to be emotionally unsuited for military service, and an additional half million were separated from active duty prematurely because of emotional instability. At the war's end there was established within the U.S. Public Health Service a National Institute of Mental Health that soon began to exercise leadership in the psychiatric field. By 1964, its total annual appropriations were of the order of $225 million. Its several programs contributed markedly to the expansion of the number of trained personnel, and further helped to shift the consensus that mental illness was largely untreatable to a more optimistic and dynamic approach.

Mental hospital care has long been the primary responsibility of state governments. In 1960, for instance, 88 percent of all hospitalized mental patients were in state hospitals, 10 percent were in veterans' hospitals, and only 2 percent were in nonprofit and private hospitals. This distribution has changed little over the past several decades, although veterans' hospitals now account for somewhat more patients than formerly. Between 1935 and 1960, the number of patients in mental hospitals expanded by 45 percent, partly because the total population increased, but also because more facilities were built and admission policies, particularly for the disturbed aged, have been liberalized. The number of professional, service, and other employees in mental hospitals has increased about twice as rapidly as the number of patients, reflecting in the first instance rising standards of professional care and in the second the utilization of more ancillary personnel because of a shortage of psychiatrists and registered nurses.

The state mental hospitals represent only a part of the major public effort to provide medical and hospital care for selected groups in the population. The Veterans Administration program represents another very large effort. Although the law stipulates that the Federal government has the primary responsibility for providing care for veterans with service-connected disabilities, when they have room, these hospitals are permitted to admit veterans with nonservice connected disabilities upon proof that they are indigent. Congress has appropriated sufficient funds to build up a system that is able to provide hospital care for considerable numbers of veterans with nonservice connected disabilities. And the criteria of indigency have never been very stringent.

Local governments also expend considerable sums for medical and hospital care primarily for the indigent. Some operate one or more municipal hospitals. Others pay for the hospital care in nonprofit institutions and occasionally even in proprietary hospitals for individuals on public welfare as well as for those who can prove that they are medically indigent. Local governments also pay for other forms of medical care—for physicians' visits to the home, clinic services, and drugs and other necessities of individuals on public welfare. A recent report by the Urban Medical Economics Research Project estimated that in 1961 all levels of government spent $530 million for health care for the residents of New York City: about $140 million was spent directly by the state and $86 million by the Federal government; over $300 million was budgeted by New York City and the remainder—about $20 million—represented collections from patients or third-party payers.

Despite the sizable hospital plants that are owned and operated by the different levels of government, it is noteworthy that the combined payments of Federal, state, and local governments to nonprofit and proprietary institutions exceed the sums that they expend in their own establishments. These payments by government to nonprofit and proprietary hospitals account for about 55 percent of all public and 13 percent of total expenditures for health and medical services.

In addition, nearly 3 million men in the Armed Forces receive complete medical care of a quality relatively few civilians enjoy. Under prescribed conditions, their dependents are eligible for medical and hospital care. The dependents are admitted to military installations or receive care under private or nonprofit auspices for which part, or all, of the bill is paid for by the Armed Forces. In recent years the Defense Department has accounted for about 2.5 percent of all expenditures for health and medical services.

Accumulating the necessary capital resources to underpin the provision of medical and health services involves a bewildering variety of institutions and arrangements. The capital of the "medical industry" includes the buildings and equipment in general, mental, tuberculosis, and other hospitals; the facilities of the public health departments; various types of clinics; physicians' and dentists' offices; nursing homes; research units; medical, nursing, technician, and other schools; and still other facilities. These facilities are owned by Federal, state, or local governments, nonprofit associations, private individuals, or business corporations. Most physicians are in private practice and own the equipment in their offices and rent or own their office space. However, nearly one-third of the total number of physicians are employed in hospitals, medical schools, governmental units, business corporations, and nonprofit health and other institutions.

The diverse ownership of hospital facilities is indicated

by statistics on the distribution of hospital beds by type of organization. In 1960, state-owned hospitals accounted for 45 percent of all hospital beds, nonprofit organizations for 29 percent, local governmental units for 12 percent, and veterans', Armed Forces', and other Federal hospitals for 11 percent. Hospitals which were privately owned and which were operated for a profit accounted for only 3 percent of the total.

These data which tell us about the ownership of hospital beds do not indicate, however, the extent to which different types of hospitals meet the needs of the community. There is a radical difference between a hospital caring for chronic patients, such as a state mental institution, and a community hospital under voluntary auspices that provides general hospital care. We can learn about the relative roles played by hospitals under different ownership by reviewing data on the admission of patients and hospital income or expenditures. In 1960, total hospital admissions amounted to 25 million. Of this number, 23 million, or 92 percent of all who were hospitalized, were admitted to general hospitals most of which are under the control of nonprofit organizations. These data point up the fact that while government hospitals play a predominant role in the care of patients with chronic diseases, the bulk of short-term care is provided by nonprofit institutions.

Modern medicine requires well-equipped hospitals and well-trained medical and ancillary personnel. Since most hospitals are not operated for profit, the question arises how are adequate construction funds obtained? In turn, what mechanisms exist to assure that the number of facilities required for the training of physicians, nurses, and other professional personnel will be forthcoming at the time when and at the places where they are needed? Since 1946, the Federal government has made sizable grants-in-aid to the states for the construction or alteration of hospitals and related facilities by the state government itself, by local governments, or by nonprofit associations. Federal funds are made available only if they are more or less matched by funds from state or local governments or nonprofit associations. The stated purpose of this Federal aid and its matching requirements has been to stimulate other public and philanthropic spending for hospitals. In addition, states, local governments, and nonprofit associations carry on their own building programs: over 60 percent of total hospital construction between 1951 and 1960 was accomplished without Federal aid.

Table 8.1   SOURCE OF FUNDS FOR THE CONSTRUCTION OF HOSPITALS: PERCENT DISTRIBUTION, AVERAGE OF 1951–1960

Item	*Percent*
Total	100
Federal funds for Federal hospitals	7
Federal aid to other hospitals	11
State and local government hospitals	5
Nonprofit hospitals	6
Other funds	82
State and local government funds	35
Voluntary	47

SOURCE: U.S. Public Health Service.

Table 8.1 illustrates the source of construction funds for hospitals and related facilities during the decade 1951–1960. We see that the Federal government provided 18 percent of all capital funds for hospitals, but less than half of these Federal expenditures were spent on Federal facilities. More than half of all funds for hospital construction were from Federal, state, or local governments. The remainder represented the contributions of philanthropy.

The training of health and medical manpower involves commingled funds and complementary actions by nonprofit and governmental units, with profit-seeking enterprise playing almost no direct role. Slightly more than half of all medical students receive their training in nonprofit medical schools; the others go to schools operated by governments. The training of nurses, technicians, and other medical personnel is also conducted in both public and nonprofit schools and hospitals. A small but increasing proportion of these personnel are now being trained in general educational institutions, such as colleges, community colleges, and high schools. Practical nurses, who were formerly trained under the auspices of private schools, are increasingly receiving training in nonprofit hospital schools and in federally aided vocational high school programs.

Of the 86 medical schools in the country, 45 are nonprofit institutions and 41 are under public auspices. There are, in addition, 6 nonprofit schools of osteopathy. Of the 47 dental schools, 27 are nonprofit and 20 are public. The nonprofit medical schools were relatively more important in former years than recently. These schools trained 65 percent of all the physicians who graduated in 1931; their share dropped to 63 percent in 1940, to 58 percent in 1950, and to 52 percent by 1960.

Partly because of this shift toward publicly operated schools, state and local governments have become the major sources of funds for the operation of medical schools. As Table 8.2 indicates, the proportion of these funds, excluding

Table 8.2 SOURCE OF OPERATING FUNDS OF ALL MEDICAL SCHOOLS: PERCENT DISTRIBUTION, 1941, 1948, and 1958

Item	1941	1948	1958
Total funds* (in millions)	$27.8	$53.5	$176.3
	(percent distribution)		
Source:			
Total	100	100	100
State and local governments	19	34	38
Nongovernment gifts and grants	36	22	19
Tuitions and fees	32	23	13
Federal training grants		4	8
General university funds†	7	13	7
Reimbursement for patient care	‡	‡	11
All other	6	4	4

* Does not include grant-supported research.
† Nonprofit schools only.
‡ Not shown separately.
SOURCE: U.S. Department of Health, Education, and Welfare.

grant-supported research, supplied by state and local governments doubled between 1941 and 1958. The other major increases were in the form of payments to associated teaching hospitals for patient care, largely by insurance plans or payments from public welfare funds and Federal training grants. Over the same period, the relative importance of funds from private sources—gifts, grants, tuition, and fees—declined from 75 percent to 39 percent.

For some time now, there has been growing concern about whether the present and prospective numbers of physicians can care adequately for the rapidly expanding population, including much larger numbers of older persons who generally require more medical attention than other age groups. In 1949, there were a total of 79 medical schools with about 25,000 students enrolled and with 5,500 who graduated that year. The comparable data for 1963–1964 were 86 schools, 32,000 students, and over 7,300 graduates.

Between 1950 and 1963, even in the absence of direct Federal assistance for the construction or operation of medical schools, 7 new medical schools were opened, and the number of graduates increased by about one-third. The total number of physicians including doctors of osteopathy increased from 232,000 to 289,000, or by about one-fourth. The population of the United States increased during the same period from 156 to 194 million, or by the same percentage. The ratio of physicians per 100,000 population in 1963 stood at 149—exactly the same as in 1950.

Obscured by this stability in the general average are the wide differences that exist among the states in the ratio of physicians to population. The twelve states with the highest ratio have between 145 to 207 non-Federal physicians per 100,000 civilian population; the lowest twelve have a ratio of between 69 to 100. The wealthier states tend to have high ratios; the poorer states have low ratios. The advocates of Federal aid to medical education see no prospect of meeting the minimum needs of the poorer states except by a substantial expansion in the supply of physicians. The opponents believe that unless other adjustments are made, the imbalances in the allocation of physicians will not be corrected.

The leaders of the American Medical Association refused to accept the widely held belief that the supply of physicians is short and, in accordance with its long-established practice of contesting any increase in the role of the Federal government in the financing of health and medical services, opposed the government's granting aid for the construction of new medical schools, assistance for their operation, and scholarship programs for medical students. Recently the AMA has modified its attitudes and now recognizes the desirability of the selective expansion of medical schools, particularly in regions of the country which are not able to meet the needs for physicians from graduates of their own institutions. Moreover, the Association no longer opposed Federal grants for construction. After repeated efforts, Congress passed legislation in 1964 which permits Federal appropriations to assist medical schools in meeting their needs for expanded plant and equipment. But the AMA remains opposed to Federal funds for operations.

We see in this episode a new dimension of the complex relations that have come to prevail in an advanced technological society between the leaders of a profession, the spokesmen for nonprofit and government medical schools, and members of the Congress. The split in opinion between the leaders of the AMA and the Association of Deans of Medical Schools about the desirability of government initiative has helped to inhibit the Congress from acting. Not until the AMA withdrew its opposition to construction grants was the legislation passed.

Although the Federal government did not become directly involved in providing financial assistance to medical schools until 1964, its large-scale expenditures for research and postgraduate training have exercised a significant influence on the trends in the profession. In 1950, 72 out of every 100 physicians were in private practice; by 1963 the ratio had dropped to 64. This 8 point difference was found in the number of physicians in training programs and in research —a combined category which increased from 16 to 24 percent. While other forces were at work, the large-scale availability of Federal funds also undoubtedly accelerated the trend toward increased specialization: in 1950 about 36 percent of the physicians in private practice regarded themselves as specialists; by 1963 the figure stood at 61 percent.

The recent widespread concern with the future supply of physicians has had a qualitative as well as a quantitative dimension. Many deans of medical schools were disturbed in recent years by the rising ratio of acceptances to applicants and the corresponding slippage in the average academic qualifications of those admitted. In part, these developments undoubtedly reflected the fact that the number of young people reaching their early twenties in the 1950s was unusually small because of the abnormally low birth rates of the 1930s. While the rapid growth of this age group and the correspondingly rapid growth in the number of college graduates have already eliminated this part of the problem, there seems another which cannot be so lightly brushed aside. Large-scale government support for higher education in the sciences, including liberal fellowship assistance and attractive careers, has undoubtedly helped to draw many potential students away from medicine. Here is just another demonstration of the subtle ways in which government and the rest of the economy interact, ways which are neither originally planned for nor anticipated.

An additional facet of the trends in manpower in the health and medical services industry should be noted. In 1900 there were just under 200,000 individuals in the health professions who were college-educated or professionally trained.

By 1960, this figure exceeded 1.1 million. The 123,000 active physicians in 1900 accounted for over 60 out of every 100 professional medical personnel. In 1960 the 242,000 physicians accounted for only 21 percent of the total.

In 1960 professional nurses accounted for about 45 percent of all professional medical personnel and about 20 percent of total personnel in the entire industry. The education of professional nurses, as Table 8.3 shows, is conducted pri-

Table 8.3 INSTITUTIONS TRAINING PROFESSIONAL NURSES, BY SOURCE OF FUNDS, 1961

Source of funds	Total	Type of Institution			
		Hospital	University or College	Junior College	Other
Total	1,118	837	191	54	36
Public	275	147	85	42	11
Nonprofit	659	526	93	7	33
Public and nonprofit ..	184	164	13	5	2

SOURCE: American Nurses Association.

marily under nonprofit auspices, particularly hospital training schools. These schools, which train nearly 80 percent of all graduating nurses, usually offer three-year diploma programs. The collegiate programs, which require four or five years of study and which lead to a bachelor's degree, are almost evenly divided between publicly operated schools and those under nonprofit auspices. The newest type of program—in junior colleges, usually a two-year program which leads to a degree of associate in arts—is overwhelmingly under public auspices.

Between 1949–1950 and 1963–1964 the number of schools providing professional nursing training declined from 1,203 to 1,142. The number of students enrolled, however, increased from about 99,000 to 125,000, and the number of graduates per year likewise increased from 25,800 to 32,400. While graduates of the three-year diploma program continue to account for the predominant number of all graduates, there has been a slow, steady rise in the number receiving a baccalaureate degree—from 3,150 in 1955–1956 to 4,480 in 1962–1963.

There has been an even more rapid relative advance during these years in the number obtaining a master's or doctor's degree in nursing—from 551 to 1,162. Federal funds have played a significant role in facilitating the higher education of some members of the nursing profession. The government's interest in subsidizing these advanced programs stemmed from its recognition that any broadscale expansion program would depend not only on improving facilities but on strengthening faculties; moreover, those with advanced degrees are more likely to pursue a career in nursing education. In 1962, slightly over half of all nurses with a master's degree or a doctorate were in nursing education.

The distribution of all professional nursing personnel by major type of employment reveals once again the crucial role of the hospital in the contemporary pattern of medical services. In 1962, 67 percent of all professional nurses were employed in hospitals and related institutions, an increase of 7 percentage points since 1954.

In the twelve years between 1950 and 1962 the number of active (full-time and part-time) professional nurses increased from 375,000 to 550,000, which raised the ratio of nurses per

100,000 population from 249 to 298. But the demand grew even more rapidly, as we see from the considerable number of budgeted positions that could not be filled and, even more telling, the rapid increases in the number of practical nurses and nurses aides. The number of practical nurses increased from about 137,000 in 1950 to about 225,000 in 1962; and the number of aides, orderlies, and attendants grew from 221,000 to 490,000.

While each of the other professional groups—dentists, pharmacists, and others—since the beginning of the century experienced sizable absolute and relative gains, the truly spectacular increases occurred among professional nurses, whose numbers grew from the unbelievably small number of 640 in 1900 to over half a million in 1960, or from a ratio of 1 nurse per 100 physicians to 208 nurses per 100 physicians.

Back of these striking changes in the shifting proportions of different types of professional medical personnel stands the expansion of the hospital and its vastly enlarged role in the provision of crucial medical services. Since nonprofit and governmental programs hold the key to the expansion of hospital services, we find here still another consequence of the growing interdependence among the several sectors of the economy. Government and nonprofit expenditures on hospitalization helped to alter existing patterns involved in the utilization of professional personnel.

There has been a considerable increase in recent years in the number of programs which provide formal training for practical nurses. This has come about primarily through the establishment of "vocational" nurse programs in state and local vocational education programs, under the stimulus of a new program of Federal grants-in-aid for that purpose. As

Table 8.4 indicates, nearly two-thirds of all approved programs for these nonprofessional nurses are provided by public vocational education programs. Most of the others are in nonprofit hospitals.

Table 8.4   STATE-APPROVED SCHOOLS OF PRACTICAL NURSE
TRAINING BY TYPE, 1961

Item	*Number*
Total	693
State and local vocational education program	438
University, college, and junior college	52
Nonprofit hospital	156
Federal, state, and local government hospital	34
Other	13

SOURCE: American Nursing Association.

The foregoing abbreviated review indicates the extent to which the Federal government has become increasingly involved in the training of medical personnel. Primarily, its involvement includes payment of tuition, training costs, and allowances to state and local health units or public and nonprofit colleges and training schools. These grants in such fields as cancer, heart disease, and vocational rehabilitation have often been associated with cooperative public health or related programs in which all three levels of government are included. The National Institutes of Health provide a variety of predoctoral, postdoctoral, and special fellowships for the training of research personnel. In addition, various programs of other agencies, including the Atomic Energy Commission and the Defense Department, provide for the training of medical personnel either specifically to help the agency meet its own needs or to add to the national supply of professional personnel.

The most recent significant shift in the public-private relationship in the field of medical and health services has been in connection with the rapid expansion of federally financed medical research. The Federal government has been involved in the support of medical research almost since the founding of the country, but by current standards the earlier efforts were minuscule. Between 1947 and 1961, total Federal expenditures for medical research increased tenfold, from $88 million to $890 million—from 32 percent to 56 percent of the total. Industry, which formerly provided 42 percent of all research funds, now furnishes only 28 percent. Nevertheless, this represents in absolute terms an eightfold growth in industry's outlays. Universities, foundations, and others provided 28 percent of all research expenditures in 1947, but only 13 percent in 1961. Although every sector increased its expenditures substantially, Federal appropriations have provided the major impetus. Indeed, the Federal government now provides nearly two-thirds of the nation's total expenditures for medical and health and related research, which is approaching an annual figure of $1.5 billion.

However, the bulk of federally sponsored medical research is carried on outside of government. In 1962, for instance, only 27 percent of all Federal medical research expenditures were actually conducted under Federal auspices. Contracts with private industry represented 5 percent and with state and local government 2 percent. Nonprofit educational institutions received half of the Federal research money, and other nonprofit institutions such as hospitals obtained 15 percent. Through this large extramural research program, Congress found a way to make large-scale funds available to medical schools. The basis for allocating the ever more liberal sums that Congress makes available has led to some striking innovations in government enterprise. The National Institutes of Health—the largest conduits of government funds in the medical field—make their grants on the basis of recommendations of panels of professionals who review the projects submitted, subject to the approval of advisory councils, which are composed of both professionals and other leadership personnel. Technically, the Surgeon General of the Public Health Service does not have to follow the recommendations of his panels and councils, but he is prohibited by law from making grants without their approval.

This pattern, as it developed, resulted in the establishment of a powerful bloc composed of the senior bureaucracy of the National Institutes of Health and the activist members of the panels. Together, they sought to expand as rapidly as possible the total sums granted by the Congress; and the principal spokesmen for enlarged appropriations before congressional committees were frequently the same individuals who were influential in the decision-making process within the National Institutes of Health. Here was a new government enterprise relying on nongovernment personnel for crucial advice and guidance about the scale and use of funds, where the advice-givers and the institutions to which they belonged directly or indirectly were the principal beneficiaries of the contracts and grants. Congressional committees recently reviewed the pattern, and while they found much to commend it, they raised questions about many issues including the development of a clearer demarcation of responsibility between the government bureaucracy and the outside experts.

To a lesser but still noticeable degree, problems also arise in the effective balancing of objectives and methods when business or foundations make research funds available to universities and hospitals. Who should take the lead in the design of the project? Who should exercise control during the course of the project? Many other bothersome issues are far from being solved.

Thus, at each level of the medical and health services industry—in the provision of services and their financing, the ownership of facilities, the raising of capital funds, the training of personnel, the conduct of research and its financing—there is a remarkable sharing of responsibilities among a wide variety of private profit-seeking, nonprofit, and governmental agencies.

The striking flexibility which has been demonstrated during the past quarter century by innovations in each of the three sectors—private, nonprofit, and government—in expanding the quantity and quality of health and medical services available to the American people must not obscure the fact that many problems remain that will require further innovations and adjustments. Indicative of the important issues are the following considerations.

The nation has not yet solved the question of the financing of hospital and medical services despite the important contributions that nonprofit and commercial insurance have made. The financing of medical services for the aged remains a crucial problem; even if Medicare or some variant is adopted, many difficulties will remain, including controlling the overuse of hospital facilities. Another serious challenge on the financing front involves the future viability of hospital prepayment plans in the face of very rapidly rising hospital costs. At some point, many people who now carry insurance may not be able to pay the required premiums. A further complication involves the competition between non-profit systems such as Blue Cross that seek to provide a community-wide service through a single rate for high- and low-risk population groups and commercial insurance companies that adjust premiums to experience and can therefore undersell Blue Cross in certain preferred markets.

The expansion of facilities and trained personnel continues to present difficulties despite the sizable contributions of various levels of government, particularly the Federal government, during the past several decades to assist in the process. The leaders of the medical profession are still not in agreement that the Federal government should contribute directly to the operating budgets of medical schools. Yet in the absence of such contributions, many private and state schools continue to encounter serious difficulties in securing the sums they need to run quality programs.

On the facilities front, unsolved problems remain with respect to both wasteful oversupply of hospital beds in certain communities and inadequate funds in others to expand capacity to a desirable level and to renovate outmoded accommodations. The accelerated flow of funds—Federal, state, local, and philanthropic—has contributed much to expansion and modernization of the nation's hospital plant since the end of World War II, but we are just now beginning to devise effective planning and control mechanisms to insure that proper balance is achieved and maintained between the community's need for hospital beds and the number and type of available accommodations. New York State recently passed legislation which stipulated that no hospital could expand its beds without prior approval of the regional hospital council. No factor is more responsible for high hospital costs than an excess capacity of hospital beds.

The very rapid increase in funds for medical research under the aegis of the Federal government has brought in its wake a series of problems the recognition of which is just now beginning. The solutions remain to be developed. Prestige follows the dollar and so does power. A relatively small number of institutions received a high proportion of all research funds, and in time these institutions were able to draw even more of the nation's limited manpower resources into medical research. As a consequence, two imbalances emerged. Bright young men shied away from practice and teaching in favor of research to a point where these other basic functions were being seriously understaffed. What is more, the heavy concentration of research grants to institutions with strong research staffs helped perpetuate the uneven distribution of strong medical centers throughout the country. Both issues have now been placed on the nation's agenda, but solutions will, at best, come slowly.

Many more unsolved problems could be identified, such as the best methods of determining the appropriate level of funding for medical research, objective determination of future medical manpower needs, new patterns of providing health and hospital services. One conclusion can be safely ventured. The solutions to these and other open questions will require in the future, as they have in the past, the constructive cooperation of the three sectors. Leadership groups in the medical and other professional societies must work in close relation with leadership groups in nonprofit hospital and insurance organizations and with the senior officials of government if constructive answers are to be found. No one sector, operating on its own, can possibly hope to come up with the solutions required for the sound improvement and expansion of this crucially important section of our economy.

9

Enterprise and Employment

This concluding chapter has a threefold objective. It will first summarize the major findings emerging from this exploratory study of the pluralistic economy. Next, it will seek to assess the impact of the recent trends upon the shape of things to come. Finally, it will consider the intensified challenge that our society will face in seeking to provide employment for all who are able and willing to work.

The single most important finding about the American economy emerging from this analysis is that surely not less than one-quarter of our gross national product is directly or indirectly attributable to the activities carried on by the not-for-profit sector, comprised of government and nonprofit institutions. Even more striking is the associated finding that not less than one-third and possibly almost two-fifths of all employment is accounted for by the activities of the not-for-profit sector. The principal reasons for the increased scale

193

and scope of the not-for-profit sector were found in the vastly enlarged role of the Federal government in connection with the cold war, the enlarged activities of state and local governments in relation to education and other community services, and the growth of nonprofit institutions primarily in the fields of health, education, and welfare.

This conclusion that the not-for-profit sector plays an important part in the operation of our contemporary economy is a statement of fact and does not imply that it is per se good or bad that this sector looms so large in the total. Nor does it imply any corollary about the alternative uses which might have been made of the resources currently employed in this growing sector. Had the not-for-profit sector grown more slowly, it is possible—although not certain—that the resources which it did absorb might have been used to support a more rapid expansion of the private sector.

Some argue that unless the not-for-profit sector continues to grow absolutely and relatively the economy at large will be unable to grow at an optimum pace. Others hold the diametrically opposite view—that an acceleration in the nation's rate of growth will be possible only if the expansion of the not-for-profit sector is contained so that the private sector can move ahead energetically. But much more is involved in accelerating the nation's economic growth than the relative expenditures and employment of the two sectors. Governmental policies, particularly with respect to fiscal and monetary matters, the productivity of research and development, the energy and capability of the private sector, and many other factors will help to determine the rate of growth.

A second finding relates to the relative rate of growth of the profit and not-for-profit sectors during the past three to four decades. The not-for-profit sector expanded relatively rapidly in the 1930s in response to the multiple problems generated by the Great Depression and very rapidly in the first half of the 1940s in response to the challenge of war. While the late 1940s saw a dynamic expansion of the profit sector, at the end of that decade the not-for-profit sector had grown relatively more over the ten-year period than the profit sector. The 1950s saw more of the same: the not-for-profit sector grew much more rapidly than the profit sector. Some deceleration of growth of the not-for-profit sector may be setting in, but more time must pass before an assessment can be made. But it is clear that since 1929 the not-for-profit sector has grown relatively more rapidly than the profit sector in terms of the labor force directly employed and in terms of the national income produced.

But a caveat is in order. By any conventional criteria—output, productivity, profits—the performance of the private sector since the onset of World War II has been good. In some years it lagged, but its record over the last quarter century is one of substantial growth; even its employment record has been good, although not fully adequate for the growth of the labor force.

Among the interesting findings emerging from this investigation was the recognition of a large number of new types of enterprise structures in the governmental and nonprofit sectors of the economy. While ours is less completely a "private" enterprise system than we have believed, the growth of our economy is still dependent on innovation and enterprise. Therefore it is not surprising to find that new enterprise structures have come to characterize the operations of both government and philanthropy.

In state government we find, for instance, hundreds of independent agencies, authorities, and commissions providing goods and services for the market, selling them above, at, or below costs, and, in many instances, accumulating large surpluses, most of which are reinvested to broaden the range of services previously provided by the organizational unit. Such new government agencies are found at every level from municipal to Federal to even international. The development of new government enterprise structures frequently involves the active cooperation of different levels of government as well as of different jurisdictions at the same levels. For instance, the Federal government has begun to share responsibility with certain states for the development of ports and water basins. There are instances of county-city agencies. There are a considerable number of bi- or multistate agencies concerned with such wide-ranging functions as river navigation, transportation, education, and health services.

The principal reason for these developments is the desire of the public for new or improved services which private enterprise is unable or unwilling to provide or which the public is unwilling to permit private profit-seeking enterprise to provide. Such services as national defense are clearly reserved to government, but other services such as transportation or power are provided at some times and in some places by government and at others by private enterprise. The Port of New York Authority was started because private enterprise balked at the financial risks involved in tunneling under the Hudson River. The fact that many of these undertakings involve very large capital outlays and that constitutional and other barriers may block their funding within the established governmental structure has led governments to find a way to circumvent these barriers through the establishment of new agencies which are in a position to borrow the capital and to pay interest out of fees so that no special burden is placed on the taxpayer.

These new enterprise structures stimulate the growth of the economy in two major regards. First, if they undertake to provide essential services, such as improved transportation, the local and the regional economy may be substantially stimulated as a result. Second, the operation, maintenance, and expansion of facilities make these structures important employers of labor and purchasers of goods and services. In this latter regard, they are likely to resemble very closely any business organization, and their contribution to current employment and output is similar. But most of the expansion of government has been through the vastly increased activities carried on by the regular departments, such as defense, education, health, and hospitals.

The public often believes that business is one thing and government is another. This was not borne out by our findings, at least not with regard to the proliferation of these new types of government agencies. They do not operate on principles entirely different from those which guide the private businessman. For the most part, these government agencies have to bid for their resources in competitive markets; they frequently have to set their charges in relation to those of others who purvey similar goods and services; their survival and expansion may depend on their making a surplus. Some, of course, were assisted by an initial grant of capital by the governmental body that established them, and all were exempted from taxes. But except for these advantages, many of them have a closer resemblance to private corporations than to conventional government agencies. The larger and better managed government enterprises have set up depreciation accounts and sinking funds; they have price structures that reflect differences in costs; they have installed modern personnel systems, and otherwise operate according to the principles of the marketplace.

Paralleling the emergence and expansion of these new types of government enterprise have been the new patterns of relationships that have emerged among government and business and nonprofit institutions. The most important, by far, has been the pattern established with respect to the major defense contractors. While these major companies are privately owned and seek profits, the Federal government exercises a great deal of influence and control over what is produced, how it is produced, the prices at which the products are sold, and the profits that the companies are permitted to retain. The multi-billion-dollar defense industry operates today under circumstances and conditions that in many regards have little or nothing in common with those that prevail in competitive markets. This is not to say that there is little or no competition among the major aerospace companies. The recent intense struggle between Boeing and General Dynamics for the very large TFX contract belies any such conclusion.

Our analysis indicated the high degree of involvement of public officials in the decision-making process in defense industries, the difficulty of developing sound criteria for judging alternative project proposals, the tentative nature of all agreements about costs and prices because of the renegotiation of profits, and a host of other considerations, all of which are more or less special to this industry. But overriding all these findings was the simple fact that a new partnership has been established between the Federal government and private business, which has made it possible for the United States to develop and maintain a highly sophisticated and dynamic defense industry that has been tested and proved not once, but repeatedly during the last quarter century.

So far our references have been to innovations in government enterprises. But we also found that innovation occurred in the nonprofit sector. The most striking developments occurred on two fronts: medical and educational services. In the field of medical care, a new structure was developed to provide insurance for hospital costs. But it was quickly expanded to include professional services in hospitals. The expanded use of hospitals brought with it a modernization of their management and personnel operations. Previously, voluntary hospitals had operated on the fringes of the money economy; now they seek to bring their charges into close relation with their costs. Few established industries have shown a faster record of growth. The voluntary hospital today is the fulcrum of the almost $40 billion health and medical services industry. The innovations in Blue Cross, Blue Shield, commercial insurance, and nonprofit hospitals together with the new relations that have come to be established between governments and nonprofit hospitals, both in paying for welfare patients and for assisting in construction, have underpinned the expansion in this sector. The crucial finding is that these innovations in the nonprofit sector have enabled the consumer to buy more health and medical services from both profit-seeking and nonprofit suppliers. Consequently, the rapid expansion of the industry has been supported primarily by enlarged private expenditures and facilitated by the new patterns of insurance. Nowhere can one find a clearer example of the interplay between innovation in enterprise structure and economic expansion.

In education, nonprofit institutions at every level, but particularly at the college and university level, have likewise demonstrated a high order of flexibility in rising to new challenges and opportunities. Several of the country's leading universities developed new organizations to cope with the very large research and development programs financed by the Federal government. Many others adjusted their conventional departmental structure to make room for a vast expansion in their research and training. Graduate instruction in the sciences was transformed as a consequence of these changes.

At the undergraduate level, many institutions which had totally inadequate endowment income modernized their tuition and scholarship structures, succeeded in securing large unrestricted alumni contributions, borrowed funds for construction from government agencies and business, and otherwise struck out in new directions in order to meet the increasingly heavy demands made on them at the very time that inflation wrought havoc with long-established income and cost structures. While private expenditures for education increased proportionately less than those for health, they were very considerable. Once again, innovation and modifications of the enterprise structures together with new relationships among nonprofit education, government, and business were the basis of this expansion. With the huge bulge in college applications still before us, further innovations must be anticipated.

While the most important transformations in nonprofit enterprise occurred in health and education services, there are a great many other examples of new activities—those carried on by trade associations, nonprofit clubs, cooperative housing ventures, community development agencies, and theatrical and musical groups, all of which contributed to quickening the economic pace.

This brief recapitulation of innovation in the not-for-profit sector would not be complete without at least brief reference to the factors which impeded the rate of the expansion. Three in particular warrant note.

In the private sector of the economy, the prospect of making a profit or higher profits is a signal that is usually, but by no means always, quickly responded to by entrepreneurs. Their forecasts may not always be correct, but the prospect of adding to their profits is likely to elicit a quick response. It is much more difficult for government and nonprofit agencies to measure and meet the potential demand for their services. In fact, when goods and services provided by the not-for-profit sector are given away or are sold at prices that are not closely geared to costs, it is difficult to apply the market concept of effective demand. A more appropriate concept would be that of "social need." But since social needs are vast and indeterminate and exceed the ability of government or philanthropy to meet all of them at any given time with the conventional resources at their disposal, the rate at which these institutions expand their operations is likely to be conditioned primarily by the willingness of the public to bear higher taxes or to make larger philanthropic donations.

The situation is somewhat different when it comes to government enterprises that do not have to wait for legislative appropriations, but can use the mechanisms of the marketplace to obtain funds for expansion. They have more latitude for expansion, but they are seldom, if ever, as free as private enterprise to respond to any and all opportunities. They operate within constraints which may set a narrow area for their activities, and they must usually obtain legislative or voter approval before expanding into a new area. Another impediment to their expansion is the fact that so many government enterprises can expand only after condemning land and buildings through the exercise of their right of eminent domain. These proceedings are seldom easy and may often turn out to be very protracted. Moreover, politicians must proceed cautiously before taking action that will result in the certain opposition of a particular minority, no matter how many benefits may eventually accrue to the community at large.

Finally, in both government and nonprofit organizations, as in the large corporation, the leadership may not rush to venture upon expansion if it means their giving up a relatively quiet and easy life for one fraught with tension and turmoil. In many nonprofit organizations the key personnel may actually oppose expansion because it might dilute their power; on the other hand, empire building is a familiar phenomenon in all large organizations, be they private or public.

These few references indicate that there are important deterrents to the accelerated expansion of enterprises in the not-for-profit sector. Both government and nonprofit institutions have been expanding in the past several decades, and each continues to expand today. But the relative growth of the sector during the past three decades implies that the forces operating toward expansion were more powerful than those which exercised a restraining influence. Without question of a doubt, the determining factor was the ability of the Federal government to respond—and to respond quickly—to the major domestic and foreign challenges.

This concludes our summary of the major findings emerging from our analysis of the transformations that have been occurring in enterprise structures in the not-for-profit sector, and sets the stage for a consideration of the parallel developments in employment. We set forth the findings related to the enterprise form first because the availability of entrepreneurial structures is the basic precondition for the expansion of employment. Unless there is an organizational structure through which an alert management is able to exploit an existing or potential demand in the market or is in a position to respond to a community need, additional investments will not be made, goods and services will not be forthcoming, and employment will not expand. The potential for the expansion of enterprise is a precondition for the expansion of employment, but unemployment can also be the cause of the creation of new enterprise structures and new jobs by stimulating the Federal government to venture into new fields.

Below are our most important findings with regard to employment in the period from the end of the New Era (1929) to the present. The number of persons employed directly in and indirectly for the not-for-profit sector in 1963 comprised at least one-third of the entire employed population; and the correct total may approximate two-fifths. Next to manufacturing, the industry which today offers the most employment is government—Federal, state, and local. Government has approximately 10 million persons directly on its payrolls out of a total labor force of 75 million. When the number of those who are employed in the private sector as a direct result of purchases that governments and nonprofit institutions make is added to the number on the payrolls of these institutions and of government, the total number of persons employed directly in and indirectly for the not-for-profit sector is not less than 25 million and may in fact be several million more.

Included in the sizable total of workers employed directly in or indirectly for the not-for-profit sector are all or a high proportion of those engaged in the provision of such basic goods and services as defense, education, health, religion, science and research, social welfare, and cultural activities—in addition to those engaged in providing conventional government services such as the post office and police.

We have also learned that the growth of employment in the not-for-profit sector, more particularly in government, did not proceed at an even pace during the past several decades. In the 1930s, because the private sector was in the doldrums, as reflected in an absolute decline in the numbers of its employees, the Federal government provided a large amount of "made" employment for those who otherwise would have been completely without work or income. The expansion of governmental work relief and related programs was such that government not only compensated for the decline in private employment during the decade but actually accounted for all of the net gains in total employment.

The first half of the 1940s witnessed a spectacular expansion in government employment, including the Armed Forces, as the country prepared for and entered a two-front war. The end of hostilities meant a rapid dismantling of the war machine, with a correspondingly large-scale expansion of employment in the private sector. At the end of the decade the not-for-profit sector had grown relatively faster than the fast growing profit sector. This trend became much more pronounced in the 1950s largely in response to the rapid growth of public employment, particularly by state and local governments. In the early sixties the pattern was continued.

The relatively more rapid growth of employment in the not-for-profit sector was a reflection of the expansion of employment by government, both direct and indirect. Much smaller but still significant were the absolute and relative increases in employment in nonprofit enterprises, among which education and health services showed the most rapid growth.

The trends in employment in the not-for-profit sector take on heightened meaning when set off against developments in the private sector. Between 1929 and 1945 employment in the private sector did not increase much primarily because of two overwhelming forces: the long depression of the 1930s and the heavy diversion of manpower to the Armed Forces during World War II. During the last two decades, a quite different pattern has emerged. The private sector has been experiencing marked growth, which has been reflected in large-scale investments, rising productivity, rapid increases in output, a good level of profits, and a somewhat less rapid rise in employment.

The total number of workers in agriculture and mining

has declined markedly since 1929. The number in transportation has also declined since 1929. Employment in manufacturing, which has increased substantially since 1929, reached a peak in World War II, during the Korean War, and in 1965. With the exception of construction, the major goods-producing industries have been characterized since 1947 by stable or declining employment. But the private sector did contribute to the expansion of employment since the end of World War II in the services—that is, through the growth of trade, finance, and a host of personal service industries.

A discussion of the role of the private sector in the expansion of employment in the production of goods and services must include brief consideration of the impact of the defense industry. During the last fifteen years—since the outbreak of the Korean War—the drift of Federal expenditures for defense has been strongly upward, although the direction has shifted several times—from ground weapons to planes to missiles to spacecraft. Scattered evidence is at hand to suggest that significant decreases in government expenditures have very unsettling effects on employment in the regions where much of the output and employment of the industry is concentrated. If the United States is, as we hope, entering a period when declines in defense spending will be feasible because of an easing in the international situation, the government will have to proceed with great caution in ordering defense cutbacks. It will be necessary to provide retraining, facilitate resettlement of excess workers, and explore alternative civilian programs in order not to undermine the economic base of the defense-centered communities which now employ tens of thousands of technical, skilled, and clerical workers in addition to those with lesser skills.

Our review revealed that a very high proportion—almost two out of three—of all professional and technical personnel are employed either directly by governments or nonprofit institutions or indirectly in private enterprises where their employment is underpinned by the purchases made by government and nonprofit institutions. In addition, government employment offers preferred job opportunities for women and Negroes. During the past seven years or so, almost all net gains in Negro employment have occurred in the not-for-profit sector. This was in sharp contrast to the earlier period, from the outbreak of World War II until the end of the Korean War, when Negroes made substantial employment gains in the private sector of the economy.

One additional fact about employment was precipitated by our analysis. The findings emphasized the unique role that the not-for-profit sector has long played in the education and training of high level manpower. Almost all the professional and technical personnel and a high proportion of all managerial personnel are college and university trained. These groups play key roles in the advancement of enterprise, on which the growth of the economy and the security of the nation so largely depend. Although nonprofit and government educational institutions have received ever larger private and governmental funds which have enabled them to expand their facilities and faculties, there are no effective mechanisms for achieving an optimum balance between our educational resources, the potential trainable supply, and the requirements of our society for professional and technical personnel. Most significant has been the inadequate recognition of the fact that the vitality of the private economy depends to an increasing degree on the quantity and quality of the trained manpower which is developed by the not-for-profit sector. The rapid expansion of the chemical, electrical, and other technologically based industries has rested on the education and training of increasing numbers of scientists and technologists. Another aspect of this relation between manpower supply and enterprise can be seen in the continuing shortages of physicians and nurses in various regions of the country, partly because of an inadequate output of trained personnel. The recent expansion in the number of medical schools and new Federal support for the training of nurses reflect a growing awareness of these relations. The availability of trained personnel is a precondition for the continued growth of the economy. The balancing of the demand and supply of trained personnel involves, of course, not only adequate capacity for training but also appropriate incentive and reward structures.

Too little attention has been paid to the difficulties that we are likely to face in the event of any leveling off or decline in the employment opportunities for highly trained personnel as a result of a slow-up or decline of governmental programs for defense and research. It has been assumed that such a decline will be matched by a corresponding expansion of openings in the private sector. However, the type of work in which many highly trained personnel have been engaged involves an order of specialized skill and competence which is not presently in great demand in private industry. The hoped-for spillover of ideas, techniques, and new products from defense to consumer markets has proved to be much slower than many originally anticipated. The private sector will probably gradually expand its research and development, but it will be more interested in hiring young graduates with broad training than the missiles experts with ten years of specialized experience.

Our major findings about the pluralistic economy can be summarized: Directly and indirectly the not-for-profit sector accounts for about one-fourth of the nation's income and up to two-fifths of the nation's employment. This sector has grown relatively more rapidly than the private sector in each of the last three decades. Considerable innovation was found in the entrepreneurial structures in the not-for-profit sector as well as in its relations with the private sector. We also found that the not-for-profit sector plays a strategic role in speeding technological advances and economic programs through its training of professional and technical manpower and its later employment directly and indirectly of two-thirds of this strategic group.

Our second task in this chapter is to distill from a review of our recent history a series of clues about the shape of things to come. This is always a venturesome undertaking since the future is always different from the past, and yet the past remains our only lead into the future.

We have noted that the prosperity that characterized our economy during the New Era (1922 to 1929) was not uniform. Relatively high unemployment and underemployment prevailed in various industries, including agriculture, bituminous coal mining, textiles, and lumbering. More significant, employment in manufacturing did not sustain an increase from the beginning of the decade. Finally, the total number of employees in nonagricultural establishments in 1928 was only 9 percent larger than at the height of the immediate postwar boom of 1920. There is more than a suggestion here that the prosperity of the New Era was based primarily on the substantial gains in productivity that followed upon World War I, gains that were sufficiently large to permit the expansion of output and profits with much more modest gains in employment. This suggests that our private economy has been unable to expand employment easily not only during the last few years but over the last four and a half decades. But this has been concealed by the significant changes wrought by the growth of the not-for-profit sector.

This means that we must look beneath the surface to identify the specific factors that have contributed to the growth of the not-for-profit sector and to assess their probable strength in the years that lie ahead. The New Deal resulted in a marked increase in the tasks that society assigned to government, including a longer compulsory period of education, increased public works, and regional development. Once World War II was behind us, this new stance toward enlarged functions for government at all levels was reaffirmed.

In addition to these and other broadened goals, government also had to cope with growing urbanization and increased concentrations of population. These developments forced state and local governments in particular to do more in order to create and maintain a tolerable environment within which more and more people could live, work, and play.

The postwar trend in national elections indicates that the American people expect to continue to look to government for broadened and improved services which they cannot otherwise secure. The growth in population and its concentration are also likely to continue. It would appear therefore that the forces that have operated since the early 1930s to increase the economic activities of government are likely to persist in the years ahead. But two caveats are in order. Firstly, the tremendous expansion in employment in public education is not likely to continue unless birth rates rise rapidly again or unless the opportunities for adult education are vastly enlarged. Secondly, the large contribution of the Federal government to employment through its defense and related programs may level off if, as we hope, the international situation eases. New programs may be fashioned to take their place, but without them, we cannot postulate the growth of the governmental sector at the same rate as in the recent past.

The situation is more cloudy with regard to the nonprofit sector. The probability of a continuing high rate of growth in all levels of nonprofit education appears likely. And this may be true also for health and medical services, although evidence is accumulating that established methods of payment may not support a continuing rapid growth. Nevertheless, nonprofit enterprise is likely to continue to grow at a rate no slower than in the recent past, particularly if government makes increasing use of nonprofit institutions in the furtherance of its several programs.

This brings us to the final considerations which grow out of this inquiry into the pluralistic economy—those relating to the challenge that our society faces in developing a balance between job seekers and jobs. Since shortly after the end of the Korean War the growth of employment has slackened. For most of the last six years, unemployment has been above the 5-percent level, in some years considerably above. Of the more than 10 million who work part-time, over 2 million do it because they cannot find full-time jobs. During the past several years the proportion of the population above the age of 14 not in the labor force has decreased by about 2 percent, which suggests that many additional persons who wanted to work have dropped out or delayed entering the labor force because of the tight job situation. The gap between the numbers able and willing to work and the number of jobs is unquestionably much wider than is reflected by the current count of unemployed.

This is the recent record. What are the prospects for the future? We noted above that despite high productivity and sustained profitability of the private sector, employment has not been expanding as rapidly as would have been necessary to employ the enlarged labor force. We noted further that we may face additional problems because the not-for-profit sector may not account for as large a proportion of new jobs.

To these portents from the past must be added another that is just coming over the horizon—that is, the sizable increase in the number of young people reaching 18 years of age. In 1965 the number will jump by one million, from 2.8 to 3.8 million, and will thereafter remain at the higher level. Unemployment rates for young people have been discouragingly high during the past several years, and they now threaten to go even higher. Moreover, the unemployment rate for Negro youngsters is appallingly high—it is about 25 percent—and Negroes now account for more than their proportionate share of new job seekers because of their higher birth rate since the end of World War II.

Other disquieting factors can be identified, such as the impact of the computer on the heretofore fast growing white-collar occupations; the rapid shrinkage in the number of starting jobs available to unskilled, new entrants to the labor force; the growing disinclination of many employers to hire youngsters without a high school diploma at a time when 30 percent of the age group are not graduating; the distance between the heart of the central city where many of the unemployed live and the potential jobs in the suburbs; the marked difficulties faced by older unemployed persons with limited education and skills. All these factors have a contemporary ring. They were not present to a comparable degree at any earlier stage of our history.

Equally if not more important is the change in national aspirations. The American public is no longer willing to tolerate a high level of unemployment. The United States cannot long maintain its leadership position among the nations of the West if its economy is characterized by a high level of unemployment, no matter how efficient or profitable its economy. Every democratic society has come to ascribe overriding importance to the maintenance of a high level of employment.

Both the Congress and the public have become slowly aware of the specter of widespread unemployment. To avoid this, primary reliance is still placed on the maintenance of a rapid rate of economic growth through appropriate monetary and fiscal policies. Recently, however, the lawmakers have moved to supplement this general approach with a wide range of specific educational and manpower programs. They have sought to strengthen general and vocational education, establish training and retraining programs, attack the causes of poverty, improve labor market mechanisms, and otherwise enhance the employability of many who are out of work or who are entering the labor force for the first time.

But the root problem—the direct expansion of the number

of jobs—has as yet been tackled only through accelerated public works and area redevelopment programs. Nor is it likely that it will be broadly tackled until a consensus is reached that it is urgent to take action. Those with jobs vastly outnumber those without jobs. Congress has been willing to pass legislation extending the period of unemployment benefits, lowering the age for social security benefits, and raising allowances to certain families in need. But it has proceeded cautiously with respect to enacting policies that might expand employment directly for fear that they might lead to a renewed inflation. Congress is apparently waiting to see how the many new programs it has recently adopted, of both a general economic and a specifically manpower nature, are working before embarking on more ambitious efforts to expand employment.

It does not appear likely that without new programs the level of unemployment will sink to an acceptable 3 to 4 percent of the labor force. The expansion of the private sector would have to be noticeably greater than it has been since the end of World War I, and particularly since 1929, to furnish the number of additional jobs that would reduce the rate of unemployment to an acceptable level. The forces that have been responsible for the rapid growth of the not-for-profit sector may weaken; at least they are not at the moment gaining strength. In the absence of new developments and with intensified competition in international trade, there is a strong likelihood that the number of persons without jobs will increase, perhaps rapidly.

What can be done? What should be done? Some argue that the United States confronts no special problem with respect to employment and that therefore nothing needs to be done beyond following policies that will insure a continuing growth of the economy in general. Others contend that we are on the verge of the new world in which the productivity of the new machines will make almost all of us redundant. All that needs to be done is to guarantee an income to each individual and family so that they will be able to purchase the goods that the new automated machines will gush forth.

Both appear to us to be extreme positions that are not supported by the facts. A more reasonable stance recognizes the existence of a problem that will probably become worse unless corrective action is initiated and maintained. We start from the premise that an adequate number of jobs will not be created automatically, nor even as a result of the new government policies that have recently been initiated. We believe that a problem does exist and in the absence of further corrective actions, it is likely to get worse, not better.

We do not believe that there is any single type of action that can assure the rapid expansion of employment. A wide range of policies are called for, and new ones may have to be devised as experience accumulates and is evaluated. We will note briefly the type of policies that appear to us to hold reasonable promise of contributing to the solution. Many of the recently initiated programs, such as the strengthening of educational, training, labor market, and other institutions involved in the development and utilization of the nation's manpower resources, appear to be steps in the right direction. We will concentrate therefore on additional approaches that are indicated by the preceding analysis.

We found that in our pluralistic economy there is a constant feedback between the growth of the private and the not-for-private sectors. Expansion in one almost inevitably stimulates expansion in the other. Therefore, a first challenge is to consider what might be done to stimulate the growth of the private sector. Three directions for action suggest themselves. The first is to shift more of the costs of innovation from the private to the public sector through government support of research on civilian products. The second is to improve the mechanisms for obtaining joint action by the two sectors so that many existing barriers to private investment can be removed. This would mean a wide range of efforts from speeding condemnation procedures for construction projects to building up strong research and development centers through the combined efforts of business, nonprofit, and government organizations. The third is to encourage the private sector through subsidies and other devices to start new enterprises, particularly in the service fields, which would use various groups of handicapped persons. We will not know whether, or to what degree, these less qualified persons are able to perform effectively in an advanced technological society unless they are given competent management and supervision. Government should seek to encourage the private sector to experiment with transferring to the service area many of the principles and methods that have been proved successful in the production of goods.

Each of the foregoing implies an experimental stance. But there is considerably more that government might do to speed enterprise and employment. There are a great many services that the public would welcome if it could obtain them at a price that is not prohibitive. These include cleaner and safer cities, more adequate educational, health, and recreational services, and expanded cultural opportunities. If government relies to a greater degree than heretofore on borrowing capital and charging fees, it will be better able to expand. But there are limits to such an approach for the reasons previously adumbrated about the difficulty of charging for services that are considered necessary for all, whether or not all can pay for them. A large-scale expansion of government-furnished services would depend to a large extent on public tolerance of higher taxes.

It does not necessarily follow that government's outlays would have to be steadily and rapidly increased. If a job creation program succeeds in shifting many who now receive one or another type of public assistance into private income-earning jobs, corresponding savings in government outlays might be possible. Furthermore, enterprises originally initiated by government or nonprofit institutions may be transferred to the private sector, as has happened to some aspects of medical services, recreation, and other fields.

The burden of these several findings is the necessity not only to remove all the barriers in the path of the expansion of the private sector, but also to reexamine every facet of the way in which government and nonprofit institutions carry on their economic activities. To strengthen their organizational structures, encourage initiative and innovation, respond to consumer needs, improve their output, experiment with new marketing and pricing devices—in short to use their resources efficiently and to remain ever responsive to the publics which they serve—are the challenges that they face.

The progress of our economy depends on the efficiency of each of its three sectors—private, nonprofit, and government —and on cooperation and complementary action among them. No sector by itself can provide all of the jobs that will be required by our expanding labor force. The nation has no option but to strive toward the accomplishment of a satisfactory level of employment. A responsible democracy adhering to its tradition and protective of its future will seek to provide jobs for all citizens who are capable of constructive work. Only such a democracy will be able to command the continuing support of its people.

Bibliography

Aerospace Industries Association of America, Inc., *Aerospace Facts and Figures 1962*, American Aviation Publications, Inc., Washington, D.C., 1962.

Arrow, Kenneth J., "Uncertainty and the Welfare Economics of Medical Care," *American Economic Review*, vol. 53, pp. 942–973, December, 1963.

Backman, Jules, *Competition in the Chemical Industry*, Manufacturing Chemists Association, Inc., Washington, D.C., May, 1964.

Bator, Francis M., *The Question of Government Spending*, Harper & Row, Publishers, Incorporated, New York, 1960.

Buchanan, James, and Gordon Tullack, *The Calculus of Consent*, The University of Michigan Press, Ann Arbor, Mich., 1962.

Dahl, Robert Alan, and Charles E. Lindblom, *Politics, Economics and Welfare*, Harper & Row, Publishers, Incorporated, New York, 1953.

Dickinson, Frank G., *Philanthropy and Public Policy*, National Bureau of Economic Research, New York, 1962.

Fabricant, Solomon, "Government and Economic Life," in *Thirty-fifth Annual Report*, National Bureau of Economic Research, New York, 1955.

Fabricant, Solomon, *The Trend of Government Activity in the United States since 1900*, National Bureau of Economic Research, New York, 1952.

Ginzberg, Eli, "Manpower Utilization in Aerospace," *Law and Contem-*

porary Problems, vol. 29, no. 2, pp. 453–467, School of Law, Duke University, Durham, N.C., Spring, 1964.

Ginzberg, Eli, *Pattern for Hospital Care,* Final Report of the New York State Hospital Study, Columbia University Press, New York, 1949.

Glaze, Thomas Edward, *Business Administration for Colleges and Universities,* Louisiana State University Press, Baton Rouge, La., 1962.

Griffin, John I., *The Port of New York,* published for the City College Press by Arco Publishing Co., New York, 1959.

Groves, Harold M., *Financing Government,* 5th ed., Holt, Rinehart and Winston, Inc., New York, 1958.

Harris, Seymour E., *The Economics of American Medicine,* The Macmillan Company, New York, 1964.

Heilbroner, Robert L., and Peter L. Bernstein, *A Primer on Government Spending,* Random House, Inc., New York, 1963.

Kaufman, Herbert, *Politics and Policies in State and Local Governments,* Prentice-Hall, Inc., Englewood Cliffs, N.J., 1963.

Kuhn, Tillo, *Public Enterprise Economics and Transport Problems,* University of California Press, Berkeley, Calif., 1962.

National Association of Mutual Savings Banks, *Mutual Savings Banking,* Monograph prepared for the Commission on Money and Credit, Prentice-Hall, Inc., Englewood Cliffs, N.J., 1962.

National Security Industrial Association, *The Impact of Governmental Research and Development Expenditures on Industrial Growth: Proceedings of a Symposium,* 1963.

New York State, *Temporary State Commission on Coordination of State Activities,* Staff Report on Public Authorities under New York State, Mar. 21, 1956.

Peck, Merton J., and Frederic M. Sherer, *The Weapons Acquisition Process: An Economic Analysis,* Harvard University, Graduate School of Business Administration, Division of Research, Boston, 1962.

Phelps, Edmund S. (ed.), *Private Wants and Public Needs,* W. W. Norton & Company, Inc., New York, 1962.

Port of New York Authority, *Latest Report—July, 1963.*

Rubel, John H., "The Impact of Governmental Research and Development on Industrial Growth: Trends and Challenge in Research and Development," in *Convertibility of Space and Defense Resources to Civilian Needs,* U.S. Senate, Committee on Labor and Public Welfare, Subcommittee on Employment and Manpower, vol. 2, Selected Readings on Employment and Manpower, 1964.

Samuelson, Paul A., "Personal Freedoms and Economic Freedoms in the Mixed Economy," in Earl F. Cheit (ed.), *The Business Establishment*, John Wiley & Sons, Inc., New York, 1964.

Samuelson, Paul A., "The Pure Theory of Public Expenditure," *Review of Economics and Statistics*, 1954, pp. 387–389.

Schultz, Theodore W., *The Economic Value of Education*, Columbia University Press, New York, 1963.

Social Legislation Information Service, *Tax Manual for Non-profit Organizations*, Washington, D.C., 1960.

Somers, Herman M., and Anne R. Somers, *Doctors, Patients and Health Insurance*, The Brookings Institution, Washington, D.C., 1961.

Stanford Research Institute, *The Industry-Government Aerospace Relationship*, 1963.

Tobin, Austin J., *The Port Authority and the Business Community*, Alumni Association, Columbia Graduate School of Business, New York, Jan. 31, 1963.

Vaizey, John, *The Economics of Education*, Faber & Faber, Ltd., London, 1962.

Weidenbaum, Murray L., "Economic Adjustment to Disarmament," *University of Washington Business Review*, 1963.

U.S. Government Publications, Government Printing Office, Washington, D.C.:

U.S. Arms Control and Disarmament Agency, *Economic Impacts of Disarmament*, by Emile Benoit, January, 1963.

U.S. Atomic Energy Commission, *Civilian Nuclear Power*, Report to the President, Nov. 20, 1962.

U.S. Congress, Joint Economic Committee, Subcommittee on Defense Procurement:

Background Material on Economic Aspects of Military Procurement and Supply, 88th Cong., 1st Sess., March, 1963. Hearings: *Impact of Military Supply and Service Activities on the Economy*, 88th Cong., 1st Sess., Mar. 28, 29, and Apr. 1, 1963.

Progress Made by the Department of Defense in Reducing the Impact of Military Procurement on the Economy, 87th Cong., 1st Sess., June 12, 1961.

Reports: *Economic Aspects of Military Procurement and Supply*, 86th Cong., 2d Sess., October, 1960.

Impact of Military Supply and Service Activities on the Economy, 88th Cong., 1st Sess., July, 1963.

U.S. Congress, Joint Economic Committee, *Subsidy and Subsidylike Programs of the U.S. Government.*

U.S. Congress, Senate, Committee on Labor and Public Welfare, Subcommittee on Employment and Manpower:
  Convertibility of Space and Defense Resources to Civilian Needs: A Search for New Employment Potentials, vol. 2, Selected Readings in Employment and Manpower, 1964.
  Exploring the Dimensions of the Manpower Revolution, vol. 1, Selected Readings in Employment and Manpower, 1964.

U.S. Congress, Senate, *Communications Satellite Act of 1962,* Report no. 1319, 87th Cong., 2d Sess., Apr. 12, 1962.

U.S. Department of Agriculture, Farmer Cooperative Service, *Farmer Cooperatives,* FCS Bulletin 1, December, 1955.

U.S. Department of Commerce, Bureau of the Census:
  Division of Governments: "Governmental Finances in the U.S. 1902 to 1957," March, 1959.
  "Governmental Finances in 1960" (annual).
  "State Distribution of Public Employment in 1963" (monthly).
  "Summary of Governmental Finances, in 1963" (monthly).
  Population Division: "Occupation by Industry," *Census of Population,* 1950 and 1960.
  "Industrial Characteristics," *Census of Population,* 1950 and 1960.
  "Occupational Characteristics," *Census of Population,* 1950 and 1960.

U.S. Department of Commerce, Office of Business Economics:
  National Income, 1954.
  Survey of Current Business, July, 1964.
  U.S. Income and Output, 1958.

U.S. Department of Health, Education, and Welfare, *Medical Care, Financing, and Utilization,* Health Economics Series, no. 1, 1962.

U.S. Department of Health, Education, and Welfare, Office of Education, "Statistics of State School Systems," *Biennial Survey of Education in Statistics of State School Systems,* 1959–1960.

U.S. Department of Labor, *Manpower Report of the President,* March, 1964.

U.S. National Science Foundation, *Research and Development in Industry,* 1960.

Index

Nonprofit enterprise, Social Security program and, 70
taxation and, 67–70
U.S. Internal Revenue Code on, 67
(*See also* Government enterprise; Health services industry; Not-for-profit sector)
North Carolina Fund, 51
Northrop Nortronics, 158
Not-for-profit sector, categories of, 86, 88
education and, 207–208
employment, indirect, from, 143–146
and net growth of, 138–142
employment trends in, 113–146, 203–205
expenditures of, 84–92
growth of, 91–111
innovations in, 193–203
scale and scope of, 82–111
summary of findings on, 209
(*See also* Government enterprise; Nonprofit enterprise)
Nuclear power, 9–10

Occupational skills (*see* Education; Employment)
Old Age, Survivors and Disability Insurance (OASDI), 137

Pennsylvania Turnpike, 39
Philadelphia Mental Health Clinic, 71
Philco, 151
Port of New York Authority, 12, 41, 196
Post Office, 38
Power Authority of New York State, 41
Pricing in nonprofit enterprise, 77–78
Profit-seeking enterprise, 2
atomic energy programs and, 48
cooperative action with government enterprise and, 45–49
employment in, growth of, 142, 205–206
indirect, from not-for-profit sector, 143–146
expansion of, 216

Profit-seeking enterprise, government as, 28
government contracts and, 45–46
government controls on, 28
government-subsidized, 4
government takeover of, 37–38
management of, compared with management of nonprofit enterprise, 74–76
nonprofit enterprise and, 79–80
operation of, 18
reliance of, on government, 28–30
(*See also* Defense contracting)
Public Health Service, 188
Public utilities, 3
Pusey, Dr., 27

Rand Corporation, 47
Redstone Arsenal, 148
Research and development, expenditures on, 102–105
Federal government and, 187
government enterprise and, 46–48, 188
manpower and, 208–209
medical, 187–189
(*See also* Defense contracting)
Research, development, test, and evaluation (RDT&E), 149
Rhode Island, government role in education in, 37

St. Lawrence Seaway Authority (Canada), 41
St. Lawrence Seaway Development Corporation, 41
San Francisco Bay Rapid Transit District, 42
Satellite communications, 49
School districts, 40
Service industry, employment in, 131–133
Skybolt program, 158
Smith, Adam, 26
Social Security Act of 1935, 172
Social Security program, 137
nonprofit enterprise and, 70

228 *The Pluralistic Economy*